W9-BNH-681

IN THE SANDS OF SINAI

A PHYSICIAN'S ACCOUNT OF THE YOM KIPPUR WAR

ITZHAK BROOK, MD

Copyright © 2011 Itzhak Brook, MD
All rights reserved.

ISBN-10: 1466385448
ISBN-13: 9781466385443

Table of Contents

Dedication v

Acknowledgement vii

Introduction ix

Chapter 1 The Morning of Yom Kippur 1973 1

Chapter 2 Gathering Place 11

Chapter 3 Getting Organized 19

Chapter 4 We are Ready 29

Chapter 5 The Long Drive South 39

Chapter 6 Too Close to the Front 45

Chapter 7 The Price of War 55

Chapter 8 Waiting in the Desert 63

Chapter 9 Aerial attacks 71

Chapter 10 Religion in War 79

Chapter 11 Fear 87

Chapter 12 Moving Towards the Suez Canal 103

Chapter 13 In the Lion's Den 111

Chapter 14 Temporary Reprieve 119

Chapter 15 On the Banks of the Canal 125

Chapter 16 My Luck Ran Out 133

Chapter 17 Evacuation 143

Chapter 18 In the Hospital 151

Chapter 19 The Aftermath 161

Dedication

This book is dedicated to the soldiers of the Supply Battalion of the 162nd Armored Division, of the Israeli Defence Forces also known as the Steel Formation who participaed in the Yom Kippur War.

Acknowledgement

I am grateful to my wife Joyce and my son Yoni for their helpful input and advice in writing this book.

The names of some of the individuals have been changed

Introduction

Over thirty-eight years have passed since the Yom Kippur War took place in October of 1973, but its impact on me has not faded. I still think about the war and relive my experiences again and again. This war posed the most serious threat to the existence of Israel in modern history and shattered conventional wisdom about the country's strengths and lack of vulnerability throughout the psyche of Israeli society. It came as a surprise to everyone involved and the army's lack of preparation and consequent delay in calling up the military reservists inflicted a heavy toll on the entire population. The only thing that saved the country was the bravery of the Israeli soldiers who sacrificed their lives in many cases to compensate for the lack of equipment and supplies. What also helped the country to regroup and turn the tide of the war was the buffer provided by the Sinai desert and the Golan Heights which delayed the advances of the Egyptian and Syrian armies. The weapons supplied by the United States to replenish the dwindling stocks of the Israeli army were also instrumental in Israel's ability to turn an initial defeat into a painful and costly victory.

I always wanted to recount my experiences during the Yom Kippur War. Even though the war only lasted seventeen days, the events changed my perspective; to this day, I divide my life between the years before and the years after the War.

This book recounts my personal experiences as a battalion physician during that time. It describes my personal experiences, struggles, fears and challenges. One of the most important lessons I learned was that war is both ugly and challenging and boasts no glory. My experience firmly convinced me that war should be avoided at all costs and should be the option of last resort. Yet, in the end, it is manifestly and sadly true that, when the survival of a nation is at stake, war may be the only choice.

I want to dedicate this book to the soldiers of my battalion who stuck it out during this horrific war. They overcame the many difficulties we faced and performed their mission, despite constant danger, as they heroically conquered their fears and anxieties. Some of them paid the ultimate price to do that. May their memories be blessed.

Chapter 1
The Morning of
Yom Kippur 1973

October 6, 1973 was an ordinary Yom Kippur – no different from the more than thirty - two others I had observed in my lifetime. The day had always been a very special one for me. Even though I was not an observant Jew, I felt the special reverence of the holiday. The significance of Yom Kippur had been installed in me by my parents from a very young age. I remember my father, Baruch, taking me with him to attend the day's prayers every year in my early childhood and I recollect the special feeling that prevailed at our home throughout the seemingly endless twenty four hours. It was the only day of the year when my mother, Haya, would not allow me to write, turn on the lights, or listen to the radio. I always felt that the world had come to a standstill on that day as I had to look back at the events which had transpired during the previous year. I truly sensed that I had to reflect seriously upon my past actions and that I was standing in judgment before God who would decide if I were to live or die in the upcoming year.

My wife, Zahava, and I and our five year old daughter, Dafna, and three year old son, Dan, lived in a two bedroom apartment furnished to us by the Kaplan Hospital in the town of Rehovot. We had a special meal on the eve of Yom Kippur prior to sunset and, as had been our custom on every Yom Kippur eve, my wife and I took our two young children with us to the neighborhood synagogue to attend the Kol Nidre prayers. As had always been the case on the night before Yom Kippur, the synagogue was very full. My father used to tell me that, according to tradition, the synagogue feels very crowded during Kol Nidre because the souls of many of the dead are also present. The ancient Aramaic prayer always made me shiver. I sensed the awe in each word as if they had a special deep meaning beyond the freedom it grants me from all previously given promises.

I was very tired on this Yom Kippur and looked forward to sleeping a little longer that morning because I had been on call for the Department of Pediatrics at Kaplan Hospital the night before. As a resident physician, I was on call every four to five nights and typically slept a long time after these nights. That day, I was awakened several times during the early morning hours by the noise of jet fighters flying overhead as they roared over the town of Rehovot – as they always did when taking off from the Tel-Nof Air Force Base south of the town. I was used to these sounds and tried to muffle them by placing a pillow over my head; I was soon able to fall back to sleep.

I had become accustomed to the jet fighters' noise over the five years my family lived in Rehovot. Moreover, I knew several of the air-force pilots and their family members because I had taken care of their sick children in the emergency room and in the pediatric ward throughout my five years as a medical resident. The pilots would often bring their sick children to Kaplan Hospital which was only six kilometers from the base. I felt privileged to be able to perform the service for these young pilots who were constantly risking their lives to defend all of us. And whenever I heard the noise of the jets, I always worried about their safety, especially during periods of tension in the border.

Those were the years of the War of Attrition that took place along the Suez Canal and the Golan Heights. The Israeli Air Force was constantly busy making bombing sorties in those areas, usually in retaliation to the Egyptian or Syrian Armies' violation of the cease fire agreement. I had learned to differentiate between bombing missions and routine flights by the sound of the jet engines. When they carried heavy bombs the planes were very loud. I could also tell by the sound the engine the direction to which they were flying. If they flew north, it was likely that a conflict was brewing along the Syrian border, and if they flew south, there was possibly trouble on the Egyptian front. In a society living in constant conflict with neighboring nations and always at the edge of imminent war, this information was crucial. I often listened to the hourly news to confirm where those planes actually flew.

This Yom Kippur morning, however, I tried to ignore the noise and kept going back to sleep, even though it occurred to me that it was unusual to hear roaring jet engines on Yom Kippur. I wondered why the air force was active during the holy day. Don't they realize this is usually "a no fly day"? I wondered. Even though most Israelis were not orthodox Jews, everyone – and everything – in the country came to a standstill on that day. I had been planning to go to the synagogue later in the morning (as I always did on Yom Kippur) but tried to sleep a little longer, sparing myself some time off from the persistent feeling of hunger.

Through the fog of sleep I heard the phone ring. It's unusual to get a phone call on Yom Kippur I thought. I'm not on call for the hospital today. Maybe the call is from one of the parents of a child that I'm taking care of. I had built a small private practice over the years and often saw sick children at their homes. I encouraged parents to call me to update me about their children's status or if they had any concerns.

My wife who was already awake and answered the call came into the bedroom.

"Wake up! You have to get up now."

I opened my eyes surprised and looked up at my wife – amazed and upset that she was waking me up so early in the morning. It was only eight thirty. Didn't she know that I liked to sleep a little longer in Yom Kippur? Didn't she remember that I had been on call on the night before and needed some more time to sleep?

"You got a phone call from your reserve battalion," she continued before I had time to protest. "There is a general call-up of your battalion and you need to be at their assembly place within an hour."

Her voice was concerned and she looked and sounded alarmed. I was too tired to digest the significance of the call right away.

"What else did they say? What's going on?"

"You'll receive a written summons within an hour, but since it's so urgent they wanted to alert you as soon as possible. The caller didn't leave more information," she continued.

I jumped out of bed as I had become accustomed to doing when being awakened for an emergency.

Over six years of internship and residency I was used to being awakened from deep sleep. I had also become accustomed to waking up and responding to medical emergencies situations instantly and was usually able to shake my tiredness within seconds. However, I never had to do so at home.

Suddenly, it all made sense to me. Everything fell into place. Fighter jet planes were flying on Yom Kippur and I was being called for duty by my battalion. This must mean that a military emergency situation had developed. My battalion had been practicing emergency call-ups for years but never on a religious holiday. Since it was Yom Kippur, I realized immediately that this was not a drill but must be a real national emergency.

I was surprised but not shaken. Growing up in Israel had made me used to living on the edge and expecting such sudden summons. It seemed that I had been waiting for such a call all my life. The threat of a sudden national emergency had been hanging over our heads at all times. However, the instant crisis was nevertheless unexpected because the security of Israel had improved immensely since the Six Day War of 1967. Despite constant conflict with the surrounding Arab countries, the risk of an all out war seemed very remote after the astounding victory of that war. Indeed, when my reserve battalion participated in large training maneuvers ten months earlier we wondered why we practiced crossing a large body of water similar to

4

the Suez Canal. It seemed so absurd that we would ever have to fight again – and even less likely to need to cross the Suez into Egypt.

All my previous calls for reserve duty had arrived weeks prior to the assigned date and I had had ample time to get ready for them. There was always enough time to take care of things I had to do, finish pending tasks, and prepare my family for my absence. However, this time was different – a real surprise. I was completely caught off guard. Yet, despite the surprise, I accepted this unexpected reality without any hesitation.

My assignment in the army reserves was as a physician for a supply battalion. I had received this assignment four years earlier, just as the battalion was being formed. This was a few months after I graduated from a medical officer training course and had been promoted to the rank of Lieutenant. I was very proud to become an officer in the Israeli Defense Forces. I had started the forty day course five years earlier but could not finish it because I had been injured in a scooter accident ten days before graduation. I broke two of the bones in my left hand and consequently had reduced range of motion in my middle finger. I joined the course a year later to complete the missing last ten days.

I had been surprised and disappointed to be assigned to a supply battalion because many of my colleagues had become tank battalion physicians. I assumed that the military had assigned me to a non fighting unit because of my permanent limited hand function. This battalion was comprised of about three hundred supply trucks and tankers. Some trucks carried ammunition, and others transported fuel, food, and water. Our battalion's task was to provide supplies to the 162nd Armored Division, also known as the Steel Formation (Utzbat HaPlada), the tank division under the command of General Avraham Adan (also called "Bren"). I had been given an ambulance in which I rode, along with my medics, at the end of the large convoy of trucks and tankers. Our duties were to take care of the medical needs of the seven hundred members of the supply battalion.

I knew that I was an integral part of the Israeli reserves which had become essential for the country's survival. Because Israel's population in 1973 included only about three million Jews and because it was surrounded by more than one hundred fifty million Arabs living in seven hostile nations, every fit male was obligated to serve in the military reserves until the age of 55. Women were also supposed to serve in the reserves but, in fact, most were excused after they married. The country's security depended on the rapid summons and deployment of the military reserve units because the standing army (comprised of 18 to 21 year old recruits) numbered only about a hundred thousand soldiers.

I had no time to digest or react emotionally to the sudden call for arms. I acted mechanically as I had been trained and put on my military uniform I kept hung at my closet. I grabbed my sleeping bag and quickly filled my military backpack with the necessary items that I might need, including my stethoscope, sunglasses, a couple of sets of underwear, and toiletries. I also made sure that I took my migraine medication. Since I had been called for reserve duty at least once a year, all of these essential items were in one place.

"Where is our map of Sinai?" I asked my wife.

Six months earlier, my wife and I had taken a five day organized tour of the Sinai Peninsula and had used a tourist map to orient ourselves. The tour was conducted by the Egged bus company and I had served as the official physician, allowing both of us to travel free of charge. Traveling throughout the beautiful and peaceful desert and climbing to the peak of Mount Sinai to see the sunrise was breathtaking. The long climb early in the morning to the summit of Mount Sinai revealed the splendor of the numerous peaks of the mountain range. As I walked up the seven hundred steps from Santa Catherina Monastery to the peak of Mount Sinai I felt connected to the events that had occurred there five thousand years earlier when Moses walked down the mountain carrying the Ten Commandments. The quiet and tranquility of the desert during that trip were in contrast to the many times when the Sinai represented a place of action and tension during my reserve duties there. It is strange, I thought, that I may be returning to this scenic desert, not as a tourist but as soldier fighting in a

war. Sinai was not only where my ancestors had wandered after fleeing their enslavement in Egypt, but a place where Israel had already
fought three wars since its creation in 1948.

Fortunately, I found the small map of Sinai and placed it in my
pocket. I had a hunch that our battalion would be sent there, as this
had been a place where our division had always maneuvered. Even
though my map did not show every road in the peninsula, I had used
it during our last training exercise and it had helped me navigate my
ambulance on several occasions. Unfortunately I did not have a more
detailed map at home, but even that one, I concluded, might prove
useful.

Should I take my camera with me? During our last division maneuvers I had taken several pictures which memorialized our experiences and, for a moment, thought that it would be a great idea to do
so once more. However, after thinking it over I decided not to take
the camera with me. I had a gut feeling that what we would be facing
this time would be something so serious and dangerous that taking
pictures would be a distraction and a luxury I could not afford. This
is not going to be fun...

I was puzzled and distressed because of the lack of information
that would explain the unexpected call to arms. Israelis were used
to living in a constant state of alertness, not knowing when the next
attack or national emergency would come. Everyone was addicted to
listening to the radio on the hour. In fact, on public buses, the hourly
news was routinely broadcast, and riders had become accustomed to
falling silent and listening attentively when the news would come on.
This was almost a necessary addiction that arose from the deep sense
of insecurity and fear of an impending disaster that had become deeply rooted in a society that could never put down its arms and relax.

Ironically, the only day of the year when Israelis were able to tem-
porarily overcome this addiction to the news was Yom Kippur. The
four radio stations and the single television station operating in the
country at that time went off the air at five o'clock on the evening
before Yom Kippur and would not begin broadcasting again until

after sunset the next day. Accordingly, there was complete information void during this period of over 25 hours, creating even greater anxiety on that day.

Meanwhile, I attempted to figure out what was happening and why I was being called up. I remembered reading in the papers a few days earlier that the Egyptian and Syrian armies had been conducting major maneuvers on their borders with Israel that week, but I could not think of anything else that would explain a national emergency. I turned on our radio, but there was only a steady whistling noise on all the four stations, the kind of static one heard from a station when it's off the air. I left the radio tuned to the army station, figuring that this would be the first one to break the silence, as I continued to pack my backpack.

Fifteen minutes later the unthinkable happened – the radio station came alive. This had never happened before on the holiest day in the Jewish calendar. The station began playing military marching music but there were no announcements. I moved the dial to listen to the other stations and in a short time they too came back to the air. A very short and cryptic announcement was delivered in a monotonous voice. The message was that the Egyptian and Syrian armies were concentrating their forces on their borders with Israel and, because of these threatening moves, the Israeli army was taking appropriate defensive actions. There were no details, no explanations – just that. It was clear to me that war was imminent. Following this announcement, the station broadcasted coded "call up" messages to reserve units. Each unit had its own short call up message that consisted of two words and each member of that unit had to report to his assembly station once the message had been broadcasted.

The continuous broadcasting of this array of bizarre list of nouns such as "green tree" or "open window" created an even stranger sensation of uncertainty. However, I was not listening closely to these codes since I already knew that I had been called up, and I kept getting ready to leave.

There was one thing I remembered I had to do on my way to the assembly location and this was to mail two letters. These were important letters that I had been working on a day earlier and I had only written them in draft form. I was in the last year of my five year residency program in pediatrics and had been planning to travel to the United States for a two year fellowship in infectious disease, after which I would return to Israel as an infectious diseases specialist. Since there was no such fellowship training available in Israel, applying for such training in the United States was the only feasible route for advanced studies. My wife and I had been looking forward to spending two years in the States. Some of our friends and my medical school classmates were already in the United States or were planning to travel there for fellowships in various medical subspecialties. Friends who had returned from similar training abroad had advised us how to organize ourselves when we arrived and were proud to share with us their slides shows showing the beautiful national parks and other sites they had visited.

I had applied to several training programs and, just a week earlier, had received letters of acceptance to two fellowship programs. After careful consideration, I elected to accept one of the two offers. Consequently, I wrote one letter accepting the offer from the University of California in Los Angeles and another one declining the offer from the University of Chicago. I chose the program in Los Angeles mainly because I had met the director of that program a month earlier when he was in Israel for a medical convention. We quickly found common ground and, after spending two days with him and his wife, I found him to be very personable, as well as an excellent teacher. Accepting an offer from someone I knew made the choice easier. The higher salary and warm weather in California were also factors that tilted the balance toward selecting that program.

I felt uncomfortable sending handwritten drafts, as opposed to formally typed replies, but I had no choice. There was no time to rewrite them, and I felt obligated to send an answer right away so as not to keep the programs in limbo. Furthermore, I had no idea when I would be back and felt that I needed to send the letters right away.

I left our apartment and walked to the gathering place, escorted by my wife and two young children. My daughter, Dafna, and my son Danny, seemed apprehensive. Even though they were very young, they sensed the seriousness of the situation. They must have picked up the conversation between me and my wife and realized that, dressed in army fatigues, I would be going away for something both important and unknown.

My daughter kept asking me questions, insisting on knowing what was going on. I tried to present to her the reality without causing her any untoward anxiety.

"I am being called by the army because I am needed to take care of the soldiers. Don't worry. Everything will be fine and I will be back home very soon."

I wished I could tell her more. The truth was, I knew so little myself.

Chapter 2
Gathering Place

It was a beautiful and pleasant sunny day. The streets we passed were quiet as they usually are on Yom Kippur. There were only a few pedestrians passing by and they were either elderly men walking slowly to synagogue and carrying their prayer books and prayer shawl (Talit) or young men walking in a hurried pace. These men were like me, dressed in disheveled military fatigues and carrying backpacks and sleeping bags. We saw no moving cars and the only sounds to be heard were the occasional rumbling of jets overhead and the noises of cars on the main street several blocks away. It was unusual and strange to hear the sound of vehicles on the normally silent day of Yom Kippur.

I took a detour so that I could pass by the red mail box. I had a strange sensation as I dropped the letters into the box. I sensed that a lot would happen between the time I mailed the letters and the time that I would receive a response. I also felt that by sending the letters I was doing something that would ensure the continuation of my future plans. For a moment my thoughts drifted to what was waiting for me next year. Just as quickly, I cut out those thoughts and concentrated on what had to be done at the moment. There would probably be a war to be fought before I could even think about any upcoming travel abroad.

As I was walking to the assembly place I felt the urge to get there as quickly as possible. I needed to become involved as soon as feasible, so that I could do my part in responding to the national emergency. I wanted to get to the front as rapidly as possible to protect my wife and children. This war would be different for me. It would be the first one in which I served as a father and the first one in which my own survival would not be paramount. This time I had to help remove the source of danger from my children.

I had never felt like this before and having the two young children walking by my side made the upcoming danger even more real. When I was younger, I used to take many physical risks and challenges without thinking twice. This time was different.

I sensed a new obligation to do my best to return home alive from this war. I was now responsible for two children who needed their father – it was not only me that I had to worry about; this time I had to do everything not to abandon my children. I sensed at that moment that this new responsibility would affect my decision-making processes – and how I would deal with upcoming risks – in the days ahead.

The gathering place for our group was a bus stop a few blocks away from my home. It was in the middle of a residential area surrounded by apartment buildings. From that location, it was possible to see the orange orchards that surrounded Rehovot. We could hear the chanting of Yom Kippur prayers from the small synagogue on the first floor of one of the residential buildings facing our assembly site.

When we arrived at the gathering place I found a few army reservists like me. A couple of active duty women soldiers were getting information from the new arrivals and were checking their names off the list of expected reservists. As time passed, more men arrived on foot and most, like me, were escorted by their wives and children. They were unshaven and some looked like they had come straight from the synagogue. Some were still carrying their prayer books and prayer shawls and had the dry lips and haunted looks that were signs of fasting. Some had red eyes and looked like they had just awakened.

It dawned on me at that moment that what was taking place was a contrast never seen in Israel. The sanctity of the holiest day in the

Jewish calendar was violated by the gathering of arms, the jets flying above, and the cars driving down the street. I reminded myself that it was permissible according to Jewish tradition to violate the holiness of Yom Kippur or Sabbath in order to save human lives. Definitely this was the situation today, I thought. This must be done so that we can survive.

We kept hearing the chanting of prayers from the small community synagogue across the street. Several elderly men, too old to be called up for the reserves, peeked at us from the windows of the synagogue. Several even came over to talk to us and inquired about the nature of the gathering. Apparently most of them were not aware that anything was amiss. It occurred to me that while these men were praying to God asking Him to grant the people of Israel life, others, including me, were getting ready to actually do it. Praying was not enough. God would help only those who helped themselves.

I customarily attended that very synagogue on the High Holidays but at that moment praying seemed irrelevant. Yet it was, in some ways, comforting to see that the tradition of prayer and observation of the holiday was not interrupted. It dawned on me at that moment that Jews had very likely been in similar situations before, when their actual survival was being threatened. The only option at those times had been to pray to God for salvation. Jewish history was replete with countless tragedies when Jews had been burned alive in their houses of prayers, the most recent during the Second World War. This is different, I thought, Jews can still pray but they can also defend themselves. What a difference having a Jewish state makes.

As more and more reservists arrived, the gathering place became crowded. I recognized some of my neighbors and friends. I saw my friend Yossi, who had just returned with his American wife from a long stay in the United States; he had not been called up, apparently because he had not yet been attached to a reserve unit. He was arguing vehemently with the army representatives and tried to convince them to take him as well, but they refused.

13

"We do not know what military unit you belong to," they told him. Yossi, visibly quite upset, could not change the situation. I knew how he must have felt not to have been called up. It was embarrassing to be left out at a time of national crisis. Men of reserve age who were not called up at a time of a national emergency often avoided leaving their homes due to embarrassment. I tried to assist him by suggesting that he call the headquarters of his old military unit to obtain instructions from them. He took my advice and left to try and contact them.

I started talking to some of the men, asking if they knew what was happening, but, like me, everyone was in the dark. Nevertheless, we were all aware that a security crisis was brewing and, like me, they were eager to get going. Within an hour, a civilian truck mobilized by the army arrived and we were told to climb aboard. I hugged and kissed my wife and children and told them not to worry. My daughter took it all in stride, as she had always done, being the oldest. However, my three year old son was quite upset and asked why I had to leave by truck and not by car. He wanted me to wait for a car. He also insisted that he wanted to come with me and cried when he was told that he would not be allowed. I silently hoped that the war in which I might soon be engaged would be the last one that Israel would have to fight and, most of all, that my son would never have to participate in the same activity.

It was a very conflicting and difficult minute for me. It was difficult to leave my family, even though I badly wanted to join my unit and be part of the fighting force that would protect them. However, the overall urge to defend my family finally overcame the difficulty of saying goodbye.

Most of the men sat on the floor of the truck (which had no benches), while a few stood up, holding the railing. The truck took off and we all waved goodbye to our families. Since the truck had no cover, I had to hold my hat so it would not fly away and faced away from the direction that we drove so that I did not get dust in my eyes. It was quite strange to be in a moving vehicle on Yom Kippur. Even non-orthodox Jews like myself avoided driving on that day so as to not to offend our observant neighbors. On the rare occasions that I had had to drive to the hospital on Yom Kippur I was nervous and apprehensive, counting on the fact that that the sticker on my windshield identifying me as a physician would spare me from the wrath of angry Orthodox Jews. Occasionally, Orthodox children would stone cars being driven on that day. However, this Yom Kippur was different; I knew that no one would be throwing stones at our car on this day.

We drove out of Rehovot, passing the gates of the Weizmann Institute of Science and the Hebrew University Faculty of Agriculture, leaving behind our home town toward an unknown and uncertain future. In the past three years, I had done research in both of these institutions and they had become a second home after Kaplan Hospital. I felt like I was bidding goodbye to them as well. I had recently finished six months of basic science research in the Weizmann Institute where I participated in cancer research. Even though this period was a required part of my residency training, I eagerly waited for the time I would be allowed to perform medical research. I was very proud when my first scientific publication (a study that had been accepted by the University of Tel Aviv as my Master of Science thesis) was published in a prestigious scientific journal. I had also volunteered for the past three years in the Hebrew University Faculty of Agriculture to teach and perform electron microscope research about the ability of viruses to cause cancer. As the view of these institutions faded away, I felt that all that I had accomplished seemed so insignificant and unimportant.

The wind was blowing hard in the uncovered truck and we were tossed up and down as we raced north through the empty streets of Ness Ziona and Rishon LeZion. We passed by the historical Rishon LeZion Carmel Winery and the central bus station – conspicuously and uncharacteristically empty. There were over thirty men of all ages in our truck. Some were in their twenties and a few were older than forty. Everyone looked concerned and tense as they reeled from the sudden change from being civilians to soldiers. Along the road were several groups of men dressed in shabby military fatigues and carrying backpacks gathering around or climbing into waiting trucks.

A few older men, sometimes escorted by young children, walked along the deserted streets carrying their prayer books.

As I looked around at the hurriedly collected group of men in the truck I was able to think for the first time about what had transpired that morning. I felt that something was not right about the whole chain of events that took place that morning. *This is not the way reservists should be called up* I thought. We must have been caught off guard by a surprise move of neighboring Arab states. Someone high up in the Israeli government or military must have been asleep instead of being on watch. This was a heretic suspicion because, like most Israelis, I had immense trust in our political and military leaders. Furthermore, the defense establishment in Israel prided itself on being vigilant and responsible – always being able to anticipate and prevent any pending hostility. It was a very unnerving suspicion that kept annoying me.

At the same time, I was wondering why we were driving north since the base of my battalion was south of Rehovot. However, I had no one to ask. The roads were almost empty as is usual during Yom Kippur, thus allowing our driver to arrive at his destination at the Bet-Dagan Metrological Station in only twenty minutes. This drive would have taken at least twice as long on a work day.

I had passed this station many times while driving on the main road from Tel Aviv to Jerusalem, but had never visited it. The station had a main building, five stories high, and a few smaller ones. There were several tall antennas on the roof of the main building and others in the compound. Scattered in the yard were numerous weather monitoring equipment that measured the speed of the wind and accumulated rain water. The station served as the main weather center for the country and apparently was used as a general assembly area for reservists from several regions.

The gravel parking lot was turned into a gathering place for hundreds of men who were immediately separated into small groups according to their battalions. Surprisingly, the place was quiet and orderly, very unusual in Israel where any gathering of people is almost always accompanied by commotion and shouting. Groups of men sat around banners naming their military units. Some rested on the ground by the shade of the few trees around the parking area as they sought refuge from the blinding sun. A few were huddling around transistor radios eagerly awaiting more information. The atmosphere was very somber compared to our practice maneuvers during the previous year. There was no joking around and friendly talk; instead, tension and uncertainty permeated the air, mixed with the reality that this was indeed a grave situation.

Things started to make sense to me as I finally understood the system behind the process of the military reserve call up. Once we disembarked from the trucks, we were welcomed by a young officer who directed everyone to his battalion's gathering place. I was directed to the site allocated for my battalion which was at the eastern corner of the parking lot. As I approached it, I was happy to finally see the familiar faces of old acquaintances. We had all spent many weeks together in the past four years training and exercising in the desert and felt like family. All of the battalion's officers had spent a social evening together with our spouses about seven months earlier at the conclusion of our last maneuvers. We had dinner and watched a show at the Hamam Night Club in Old Yaffo, further consolidating our battalion's unity.

Under normal circumstances we would have welcomed each other by shouting, hugging, and inquiring about what had transpired in our lives since we had last seen each other. However, this time was different. We did not exchange more than a few cordial words and set down on the gravel waiting for the next order. This attitude was the result of the exhaustion we felt from fasting and the sensation that something serious was going on. Based on the limited exchange of information and sharing of speculations, we developed a growing realization that somehow what was transpiring was the result of negligence on the part of both the civilian and military establishments.

As we sat waiting anxiously, rumors and bits of information started to spread. Some heard that the Syrians had invaded the Golan

Heights and bombed Israeli air force bases. Others said that the Egyptians had bombed Israeli military bases in Sinai. The radio station kept broadcasting military marches and cryptic military call up codes, but no news. Finally, the radio stations began broadcasting more details. There was silence in the parking lot when the news came. The message became clearer. Two Arab countries were gathering their armies and were getting ready to attack Israel on two fronts. Egypt was poised in the south and Syria in the north. The expected time of the attacks was six o'clock in the evening.

I looked at my watch; it was eleven in the morning. We had only seven hours left to do something to stop them. Could we? Was it too late? We were not even at our battalion's base. Why were we in the center of the country and not at the front with our tank division? Even though I was a member of a supply battalion, I knew that we were an essential part of the tank division that was critical to Israel's ability to stop an imminent attack.

Chapter 3
Getting Organized

The order to move finally came at noon. Two dozen members of our battalion boarded a civilian truck with seats facing each other; we were off to our own base. All of our trucks and supplies, including all of our medical equipment, were stored at that military base about twenty-five kilometers away. This time the truck transported only those individuals belonging to our battalion. Since the truck was uncovered and speeding forward, I felt the wind blowing all the time. I did not mind the chilly wind though, because I wanted to get to our base as quickly as possible — I felt a sense of urgency as if getting there sooner would make a difference. The ride was particularly fast because the roads, usually jammed with traffic, were still quite empty.

We drove back on the same road we had taken that morning, again passing through Rishon Lezion and Rehovot. The towns seemed to be busier than they had been a couple of hours earlier and more people were walking in the streets. After reaching Rehovot we proceeded south toward our base. I was frustrated realizing that we had wasted over three hours traveling north – only to return in the opposite direction. Thirty minutes after we departed, we finally arrived at our base south of the town of Yavne. It felt good to finally see the gates of our base open for us. We were finally a step closer to getting to the front.

The military camp was large and had several rows of one story barracks with multiple storage facilities – enough to equip a supply battalion with all its needs. It was an old base that had been built by the British over thirty years earlier. Despite its age, it was well maintained and sparklingly clean. The administrative barracks were surrounded by decorative bushes and flowered plants, which, in turn, were surrounded by white painted bricks. A superficial look would not reveal to an untrained observer that the base held tons of ammunition, gasoline, and other supplies, as well as more than two hundred vehicles to transport them. Dangerous supplies were stored in well-hidden underground bunkers at the back of the base.

The place was very noisy, constantly humming with vehicles and personnel. People were shouting at each other, giving directions or issuing orders. Trucks and other vehicles were arriving all the time; they unloaded reservists who were immediately directed to their respective units by individuals awaiting each truck. Every reservist arrived, as I had, with a small backpack and a sleeping bag, already dressed in military fatigues. Streams of individuals headed in different directions, but most had a determined look in their eyes, as if they knew exactly where they were going. They carried their personal equipment, plus a rifle and a helmet. The repeated maneuvers that we had done seemed to pay off. There was a purposeful attitude to the commotion and the seemingly chaotic atmosphere. People were executing a well rehearsed program of mobilization. New arrivals were given essential military equipment for which they had to sign and were immediately sent to their individual companies to assist in the mobilization of the battalion.

At the storage areas, boxes of equipment and supplies were being loaded into trucks. Most of the loading was done manually by soldiers who formed a human chain from the storage areas to the trucks. They handed these boxes from one person to another as rapidly as they could. Seeing this scene reminded me of what I had gone through during the 1956 Sinai Campaign. I was fifteen years old and a high school student at the Hebrew Reali School in Haifa. My class had volunteered to assist the military effort by loading trains with boxes of military supplies and food rations. These trains were to transport supplies to the Israeli troops fighting in the Sinai Peninsula. We spent hours at the supply base at the slope of the Mount Carmel Beach (Hof HaCarmel) near Haifa, passing boxes to each other from military trucks onto the waiting train wagons. I remembered that we felt keenly disappointed that we could not do something more meaningful to contribute to the war effort – but were nevertheless proud to have at least done something.

At some loading areas forklifts moved heavy containers of ammunition into trucks loading them to capacity. In another area, long rows of trucks, vans, and jeeps waited at the gas station to be refueled for the trip south. Drivers filled up extra gasoline containers with fuel for the long trip. Many of these vehicles were civilian that had been drafted to supplement the military transport. The civilian vehicles were an anomaly, an array of various models painted in a multitude of different colors. The military did not have sufficient vehicles to carry on its mission and instead heavily relied on civilian vehicles to bolster the reserve units. Even though the military paid the owners for the time their vehicles were used, I felt sorry for the owners because the wear and tear on these vehicles far exceeded the compensation received. Moreover, military drivers were far less attentive to the needs of these cars than their owners would be. At that time, cars were a luxury relatively few people could afford, primarily because of high taxes. I would not have been happy if my personal car had been commandeered by the military.

As soon as we dismounted the truck we were directed to get our personal supplies and equipment. Because I had been to that base only ten months earlier during our divisional maneuvers, it was easy for me to find my way, and I knew what I had to do to obtain my personal equipment and the medical supplies needed for the operation. I first went to the armory to receive my personal weapon. The armory was in a large cellar and, as I arrived, I saw rows of rifles and submachine guns lined up on wooden railings. The place was dimly lit and reeked of the familiar heavy smell of the oil used to lubricate weaponry. I had no idea what weapon I would be receiving and was relieved to be issued an Uzi submachine gun – both effective and light-weight. I also received two cartridges of ammunition for the gun, a helmet, and a personal anti-nerve gas syringe. Because of the uncertainty about exposure to nerve gas, this was a standard item distributed to every soldier.

The smell of lubricating oil emanating from my Uzi assured me that it had been properly stored. I wiped the excess oil with a piece of cloth, being careful not to stain my uniform. I had long ago learned to treat any weapon with a lot of care and respect, knowing that my life may depend on it. Growing up during the British Mandate in then Palestine, where the Jewish population, subjected to unprovoked attacks from Arabs, were forced to hide their weapons from the British authorities, made me appreciate the freedom to openly having a weapon to defend myself.

I clearly remember an episode when British paratroopers (the Kalaniyot) searched our apartment in Haifa for hidden weapons during "Black Saturday" in 1946. This was a Saturday where the British army and police imposed a curfew and systematically searched homes for Jewish underground fighters and their weapons. I was afraid that the soldiers would confiscate the toy rifle my father had made for me. Sure enough, that afternoon two tall armed soldiers, wearing red berets and the uniform of the British paratrooper, knocked on our door and politely asked my mother if they could come inside. I stood behind my mother holding my toy gun and, before the soldiers could explain their mission, blurted out angrily, "You can have it," as I thrust my little rifle toward them. I felt anger and resentment at being at their mercy and contemptuously handed them the toy gun. Although these British soldiers likely did not understand my Hebrew, they were visibly taken aback by a five year old who didn't want to be in trouble with the law. They politely refused to take my proffered "weapon" and, after giving our apartment a brief search, left empty-handed.

The Uzi I had been issued was an old model with a wooden handle. Before signing for it I tried to see if it functioned well without ammunition and pressed the trigger several times. The hammer made a snapping sound as it hit the empty barrel. Although the weapon looked like it had had years of usage, it seemed to be in good shape. Having a personal weapon gave me a deep sense of security. I knew that I would keep this Uzi with me at all times in the coming days. This attitude had been bred in me by my past military training. One never leaves behind a friend or a weapon.

I was also happy to receive the Uzi because during the last divisional maneuvers I had only been given a Colt revolver with a meager supply of five bullets. Even though I protested this miniscule supply of bullets, I was not successful in obtaining additional ammunition. Despite the convenience of always carrying a revolver in a holster on my belt, I often felt insecure because, on many occasions, it was the only weapon in our ambulance. Since we had to travel long distances in the Sinai desert by ourselves, I wished that I had a more effective weapon. At that time, although the Sinai was controlled by Israel, it was also sparsely inhabited by Bedouins whose loyalties were to anyone who paid them more than the next person. A painful reminder of how dangerous the desert could be was an incident that had occurred about a year earlier. Three weeks before our maneuvers, a mine that had been placed by a local Bedouin killed two of my medical school classmates. They had been driving through the desert, preparing for the upcoming maneuvers, when they were killed. One had been a very good friend. I painfully remembered attending their funerals along with many of our classmates. It was later discovered that the Egyptians had paid the Bedouin fifty dollars to place the mine.

Although I was a physician, I was very much aware of also being a soldier – and that I would be seen as such by our enemies. Although international rules prohibited firing on a medic or an ambulance, these rules of warfare were rarely followed by our adversaries. And even if they adhered to these rules, it was often difficult for the enemy to distinguish a medical caregiver from an ordinary soldier. I knew that I might have to use my weapon to protect myself and my fellow soldiers. I was determined to use it when and if needed, and my training in my youth and in the army gave me the self confidence to do it. I had excelled in sharp shooting and having a gun by my side had given me a sense of security in the past. I had a feeling that this time having an Uzi submachine gun would be important.

I was very much aware of the conflicts and contradictions I faced as a physician in war. I was trained to save lives, yet in the battlefield I could find myself in situations in which I needed to take a life in order to survive. I did not like the idea of doing harm to others, but I knew that if I were ever in a situation where I had to shoot, I would do so without hesitation. However, I also knew that I would immediately try to assist and care for any enemy soldier that I might harm. In fact, during the Six Day War in 1967, I cared for many enemy soldiers. The war had broken out two weeks before the end of my last year at Hadassah Medical School in Jerusalem. I had worked as a nurse in the emergency room of the Hadassah University hospital for the past two years to earn money and I was stationed at that hospital when the war started. During the first 72 hours we took care of over five hundred wounded soldiers and civilians, among them many Jordanian and Egyptian wounded prisoners of war.

Even though I had mixed feeling about caring for the wounded enemy soldiers, I saw them first and foremost as human beings in need of help. Many of these wounded soldiers were visibly scared to death when I approached them. I could see the fear in their eyes, as if they expected that I would harm them. I wondered if their fear was based on knowing what they would have done to me should I have been a prisoner of war. I also assumed that years of anti-Israeli propaganda depicted us as monstrous and cruel people. Most of these soldiers were tense and apprehensive throughout the treatment and looked in disbelief as we Israelis worked to care for their wounds. Even though it was emotionally difficult for me to provide care for enemy soldiers, I was proud that I could overcome my anger and treat these individuals as I would have wanted to be treated in a similar situation.

"Hi Doc – I can see that you already got an Uzi."

I peered in the direction of the voice and saw one of my medics, Ehud, who had also arrived to receive his weapon.

Ehud was my deputy head medic; I was glad to see him.

"Are the other medics already here?" I inquired.

"Everyone is here except for Yossi," he responded.

I was relieved and empowered to learn that four of my five medics had arrived, knowing that we could function well as a cohesive group. The recent maneuvers had strengthened our ability to perform under pressure.

I waited with Ehud until he received a Czechoslovakian rifle, the standard weapon issued to all the soldiers in the battalion. A World War One vintage rifle that had served Israel well throughout the previous twenty-five years, it was a heavy single shot rifle with only a five bullet magazine – and it had to be reloaded manually after each shot. This was no match for the modern automatic Kalashnikov rifles carried by Arab soldiers. I felt sorry for Ehud, for I knew that carrying such a heavy weapon, while caring for the injured, would be extremely difficult – but there was nothing I could do about it. We were a supply battalion, not expected to participate in the fighting, and Israel's limited supply of modern rifles was to be distributed only to combat troops.

Within a short period of time I met the other three medics. They were in their early twenties, a little younger than the average age of the soldiers in our battalion who were in their late thirties and earlier forties, and had finished their compulsive military service two to four years earlier. I was happy to hear that my medics had made it because I had learned to count on them in delivering care for the troops. They already knew many of the soldiers, making our health care delivery smoother. Over the years of training I had gotten to know each of the medics very well and could recognize their individual strengths and weaknesses. I had developed friendships with some of them and learned to trust their ability to perform well, even under challenging circumstances.

I was disappointed, however, to hear that Yossi, our head medic, would not be joining us. Being one man short would make the task of providing adequate care for the seven hundred men battalion even more difficult. We would each have to work harder to compensate. Avner, another medic who was in touch with Yossi, told me that he had gone to Spain to visit his family for the High Holidays and had not yet returned. I was sorry not to have Yossi with us. He was a customs agent in his civilian life and an efficient and reliable head medic.

Ehud was the most level headed among the medics and I asked him to take over the task of heading our team. As a sergeant and the highest ranking medic, it was a natural role for him to assume. He was a third year law student, serious and realistic, and had always kept his objectivity and rational thinking, even in stressful situations. I felt that with his leadership we would have a smooth operation.

Thin, sensitive, and shy, Avner was newly wed and in the business of selling music albums. Because of his emotional vulnerability, I treated him more gently than the other medics. I knew that he was struggling to establish himself in his business and was happy to learn that he was doing much better financially after a long period of hard work.

The other two medics, Zvika and Shmuel, were religiously observant. They wore knitted yarmulkes (kippas), always performed the required religious rituals meticulously, praying in the morning and, whenever possible at dusk, and always recited a blessing before each meal. Zvika, a second year engineering student at the Technion School of Technology in Haifa, was the more observant. He had a very determined personality, with strong convictions on a variety of topics. And although he generally kept to himself, he often got into philosophical arguments with me about moral and ethical issues – and would never compromise his stand.

Shmuel, who was married and worked as a supply clerk in a large company, was very pleasant and friendly, eager to help anyone in need. He had a "can do attitude," which prompted me to assign him difficult and delicate tasks. His patient skills were excellent and he was able to explain to our patients the rationale for suggested treatments, even when they were not the ones desired. He also had great managerial talents and kept our records and supplies in order.

Joining us for the first time was Avi, who was in his early thirties and was assigned as our ambulance driver. I could see that he had some difficulty blending into our close knit group and hoped that he would feel more integrated over time.

Chapter 4
We are ready

We proceeded to the barracks where our supplies and medical equipment were stored. A tall and skinny active duty clerk welcomed us and directed us to carry out the items we were to receive. The items were stored on shelves in a large warehouse along with other material destined for other purposes. We were expecting to receive the same six large wooden containers that we had used during our previous assignments. These contained medical supplies and equipment sufficient to care for our seven hundred member battalion. This time, however, there were only four such containers reserved for our use.

Ehud, Shmuel, and I sat among the containers and reviewed each of their contents very carefully. It became clear that our supplies and equipment were deficient in both quantity and quality and did not include all the items we had received in the past. We were missing sufficient intravenous infusion bags and sets, bandages, and medications, as well as enough intubation and resuscitation equipment and suction machines. I was upset to see these deficiencies because I was afraid that we would need all of these items, especially since we were potentially facing many injuries.

"Why can't we get the same items we had before?" I protested. "We need all the boxes to take care of our battalion!"

The clerk shrugged his shoulders, responding indifferently, "This is what is here for you. I have no idea where the other two containers are."

It was clear that there was nothing I could do about it. Someone had not done his job correctly and failed to store and maintain our supplies.

This is clearly blunt negligence that may cost us lives! How can someone fail to maintain the battalion's supplies?

Unfortunately, it was not only medical supplies that were missing, but, as we were to learn, other important pieces of equipment were not to be found. Going to war ill-equipped is a handicap.

Reluctantly, I had to accept that we had to do with what was available. There was no time to look for missing supplies and no one to complain to. We took the containers out and the medics and I spent the next three hours familiarizing ourselves with their contents so that we would know where to find each item when we need it. I made sure that the instruments needed to introduce a tube to the trachea (laryngoscopes) and ventilate a person worked fine and had good batteries. I also ascertained that all of our flashlights were working. We reviewed the medications in the containers to ensure that we knew what was available.

As expected, my supplies were limited but sufficient to cover the most common conditions we might encounter in the field. It was reassuring to confirm that every class of medication was represented by at least one drug. I made sure that we had the essential intravenous fluids that would be needed for seriously injured individuals. I also made sure we had enough medications to deal with severe pain and required that my medics each carry a few narcotic drugs and anti-chemical war agent ampoules in his pockets. We augmented each medic's backpack with extra supplies so that he could act independently to care for severely injured individuals should we become separated. Remembering the biblical story of how Yaakov split his convoy in two when he planned to meet his brother Esav, I kept one container with us and placed the other three in separate vehicles so that if one vehicle was lost we would not lose all of our supplies.

The last important item of preparation was to make sure that the medics knew how to operate the equipment. We practiced the use of the suction machine and oxygen delivery system. I also briefly reviewed with the medics what we would do in case of mass casualty and how we would triage the injured.

To our great disappointment, we were not assigned an ambulance as we had received during our previous maneuvers, but were issued a drafted civilian commercial van that we were expected to quickly retrofit with essential equipment and supplies. The military ambulance we had used before was a Willys four wheel drive vehicle, painted in the Army's brown and could exit the main road and travel in sand and other difficult terrain. It was well out-fitted and contained all the medical equipment needed to care for the wounded, including oxygen and suction outlets, bright surgical lamps, and four stretchers. It also had plenty of storage areas and cabinets for essential equipment and supplies.

In contrast, the civilian van we received was much smaller, without four wheel drive capability or any of the above amenities. The van had been painted blue and had no signs to distinguish it as a medical vehicle. This particularly concerned me, because such a vehicle would stand out in the desert and thus could be easily targeted by the enemy. I inquired about getting a camouflaging net to cover the van but none was available. An idea occurred to me as I looked around and saw vehicles covered with dirt – why not create our own dirty vehicle? I quickly decided to change the color of our van by improvising camouflage. I instructed my medics to hose the van with water and then dust it with soil. Once the soil dried, the van looked the same brownish-yellow color of the soil and thus blended well in the terrain. I was not sure how this "camouflage" would last, but figured that, if necessary, we could repeat the "painting" again.

The van would become our second home in the ensuing days. It carried all of our urgent medical supplies while the rest of our equipment and supplies was placed on supply and command trucks behind us. We made sure that we had several large drinking water containers (jerricans) and enough food ration boxes. We fitted the van to carry two stretchers and arranged it so that there were places where we could situate intravenous liquids, oxygen tanks, and other essential emergency equipment. However, despite all our efforts, it was a poor substitute for a real ambulance.

Having a civilian vehicle meant that we also had access to a car radio. We kept anxiously listening for any bits of news. Even Zvika and Shmuel, the religiously observant medics, did not protest our decision to leave the radio on during Yom Kippur. Considering the arguments we had in the past – especially with Zvika about observing the Sabbath – this was a change. We considered the radio to be our lifeline for information as no one was providing us with any updates about the war.

Finally, at two fifteen, came the ominous news – the Egyptian and Syrian armies had attacked. Apparently, the earlier estimate that the war would begin at six p.m. was incorrect. Egyptian soldiers were crossing the Suez Canal and attacking the Israeli defense line in the south, while, at the same time, the Syrian army was attacking in the Golan Heights to the north. According to the radio announcers, the Israeli army and air force were fighting back and blocking the advance of the enemy armies. A short time later, the alarm sirens came on and we could also hear distant sirens in the town of Yavne, a few kilometers away. The War had started. I wondered what the war would be called this time. Would it be referred to with a glorious name such as "The Six Day War" that indicated how quickly we were victorious – or would it be given a name that would forever associate it with a defeat?

In the past, the sound of sirens was usually a sign that an aerial assault was imminent. This time we had few shelters in the camp and certainly not enough for the seven hundred soldiers in our battalion. Hearing the alarm sound was unnerving.

" *Why is there an alarm? We are very far away from the fronts and our enemies' air forces can't possibly penetrate our aerial defenses and reach the center of the country. This must mean that our situation is not very good and we are even under threat far away from the fronts.*"

Although the sound of sirens suggested that we might be vulnerable to enemy attacks, I was still very confident in our military superiority. I looked around and no one seemed to alter what they were doing. Like me, everyone seemed to ignore the sirens and did not seek shelter, going on with their business as if nothing had happened.

I must have developed some tolerance to the sounds of the sirens because I had been exposed to them at a very young age. Growing up in Haifa during the Second World War, I experienced repeated alarms whenever Italian air force planes came from Lebanon to attack the oil refineries and harbor in the city. I had become so used to these alarms that I often refused to go down to the shelter, causing untold aggravation on the part of my worried mother.

As the hours passed, we were able to get more and more organized. New reservists kept arriving and the base became increasingly crowded. I saw a greater number of people that I knew from our past maneuvers, making a stressful atmosphere strangely more friendly and hospitable. I did not have much time to talk since we were all busy getting ready to leave as soon as possible.

There was no small talk; everyone was somber and serious. The gravity of the situation was palpable, and fear and uncertainty for the future were the unspoken sentiments on everyone's face. The only one who kept positive attitude was Shmuel, who openly expressed his optimism, telling us "Things will work out. We will win again with God's help." *It was good to hear him say this,* I thought. *I wish I could believe, as Shmuel obviously does, that God's help will be enough this time.*

Our battalion had twenty two female soldiers who held clerical, communication, and administrative positions. Their numbers were small because most women had been excused from the reserve duty once they were married or had children. The presence of females in our battalion was, however, very important. Not only did they perform important duties but their presence boosted the moral of the men. During previous exercises I noticed that men paid greater attention to their uniforms and appearance, nor did they complain as much, when females were around. The thinking among the men was that if the women soldiers can endure the hardships, so could they. Women soldiers rarely came to me with medical problems and when they did it was always because they had a genuine one. Men, on the other hand, often asked to be discharged from the battalion's exercises for sometimes flimsy excuses.

Although I was happy to see that most of the women in our battalion had arrived, I also felt apprehensive about their safety should we be under direct threat. Strangely, I felt more protective toward the women soldiers, mostly because they could be more vulnerable to hostilities, especially if we would be under combat. I was worried that they would not be able to physically defend themselves and that they would be subject to abuse and rape should they fall prisoners of war.

To my surprise, none of the reservists came to look for me because of any medical problems. This was not my experience in the past when our battalion had been called up for maneuvers. In all of these instances, I was constantly besieged by men who asked to be excused from participating in the planned training. A few had legitimate medical excuses, such as uncontrolled high blood pressure or recent serious surgery, for which I excused them after reviewing their medical records and verifying their conditions. Many of the soldiers, however, were trying to be excused because of personal reasons and used medical reasons to justify this. For example, I was frequently confronted with complaints about vague muscle or joint pain, and missing glasses.

I had never liked be placed in a position where I had to determine who could leave and who would stay. I tried to do my best to separate those who were malingering from those who had true medical conditions. Over time I became better in distinguishing between the two and earned a reputation as someone who could not be fooled. My medics were also very helpful in sorting out those looking for a way home from those with a true medical problem.

I assumed that the reason none of the soldiers wanted to leave was because this time, it was the real thing. Like me, they must have felt that they wanted to do their part in protecting their families and their country. I was very proud of our battalion's soldiers who must have ignored any medical problem they might have had. The few individuals who came to us seeking assistance were those who forgot some of their personal medications at home or who needed medications for headache or cold.

Late afternoon came and a couple of the soldiers started distributing loaves of bread. A local bakery from Yavne sent several large baskets full of freshly baked black bread. It was still warm and the smell of the bread was intoxicating. When I saw the bread, I momentarily forgot it was Yom Kippur, a day of fasting. When I observed the bread passed down a line of people who refused to eat it, I remembered what day it was. While some people succumbed to the temptation and ate a slice of bread most people elected to overcome the urge to eat before sunset and continued to observe the traditional fasting. I could not blame anyone who chose to eat and, although I chose not to, I encouraged everyone around me to eat. After all, we were at war and would need all of our strength to carry out our tasks. Fasting was harder when one has to work as we did.

Evening came and we were still busy getting organized. It was not clear when we would leave the camp on our way to the front. The radio stations did not provide much information and repeated the same message: the Israeli Defense Forces were blocking the attacks by the Egyptians and Syrians. Groups of soldiers huddled together to pray the Yom Kippur evening prayers which concluded the fast. They stood in groups facing Jerusalem in the east, at different locations in the camp. Some prayed moving back and forth, wearing prayer shawls and holding prayer books. Most, however, joined in the prayers, devoid of prayer shawls and prayer books, as though they needed to turn to God not only because of Yom Kippur, but because we were facing an uncertain and difficult time. These were spontaneous assemblies of men which illustrated the deep meaning of Yom Kippur to the Jewish people. I thought about joining the prayers but decided against it because we were still busy familiarizing ourselves with our medical equipment and supplies.

After sundown we were given boxes of field food rations to break the fast. However, we were not sure when the holiday was actually over and when it was permissible to eat again. We resorted to using the ancient tradition of looking up at the stars to ascertain when two stars could be observed. Fortunately, there were few clouds in the sky and when we finally observed the stars we opened the food boxes and ate. It was a relief to be free of the annoying sensation of hunger and thirst and feel the surge of energy that followed our repast.

We were not sure when we would be ordered to depart the camp to the front. No one could give me a clear answer. Such an order would probably come from our divisional headquarters. As the hours passed without an order, it seemed that we would be spending the night at the base. This was personally disappointing and frustrating because I was eager to get going as soon as possible. However, I realized that, as a supply battalion, we would not be among the first to be dispatched to the front. Tank battalions and other essential elements of the army would have a priority and would probably be sent earlier than us. We would likely be sent later so as not to crowd the narrow roads.

We all found places to lie down in our sleeping bags and get some sleep, not knowing if and when we would be told to move. I decided to spend the night inside our improvised ambulance lying on a stretcher and, after a short time, was able to fall asleep.

I woke up several times during the night because of the noise around me. Trucks kept passing by and soldiers were busy unpacking equipment and loading their vehicles. Morning finally came and, after a while, we learned that our battalion was scheduled to leave around noon. Since we had already finished our preparations and since there were five hours left before our departure, I thought I could drive home and say goodbye again to my wife and children, letting them know that I was all right. I felt that my departure the day earlier was too abrupt and likely upset my children; I hoped that if I returned soon, it would reduce their anxieties. Because my home was only twelve kilometers away, it seemed feasible to make the trip.

I got my commanding officer's permission to leave for a couple of hours and also informed Ehud about it. I took off in a communication jeep that was part of our battalion, taking with me only my Uzi and a loaf of bread I had picked up before leaving the camp. The roads were much busier compared to the traffic on the previous day, but I made the trip within a short period of time. I parked the jeep by our apartment house and quickly climbed the three floors to our home.

I opened the door into my apartment as my wife was serving breakfast to the children. Everyone was surprised and happy to see me walk in, as they had not expected to see me so soon. They were tuned to the radio that was breaking the recent news from the fronts. The children were still wearing their pajamas and looked very tired. I was happy to see my family again and gave my wife the loaf of fresh bread that I had brought. I was not sure if there would be any bread delivery in town because of the state of emergency and felt better that they had some fresh food. My wife told me of a long night during which they spent several hours in the building's bomb shelter along with the other neighbors. All of the men in our building were gone; they had also been called up to the army. The only exception was the neighbor who lived in the apartment below us who was in his sixties. However, his two sons, one a paratrooper and the other a tank crew member, had been drafted.

My wife's classes at Tel Aviv University had been cancelled, as was our children's kindergarten. My younger sister, Zipi, who was studying to become a laboratory technician in Tel Aviv, would be coming to stay in our home. She had been excused from military service and allowed to finish her studies because both of our parents had died several years ago. Her boyfriend, who was recently discharged from active duty in the Communication Corps, had been called up like everyone else. I was glad that my sister would be coming over, so that my family members would be able to stay together and care for each other at this critical time.

Within minutes of my return, my wife told me that she wanted to use my unexpected arrival to go to the grocery store to get some essential food items while I watched the children. I was disappointed that she did not realize that this was a precious moment – it could have been the last time that we would be together as we faced an uncertain future. It also occurred to me that should something happen to me, this would have been the last time I would see her. She left before I had time to protest. I sat down with my children on the floor of our living room and spent the next half an hour explaining in simple terms what was happening. Even though I was tense and rushed, I tried to be truthful but also non-alarmist.

"There is a war going on now and Israel is being attacked by two Arab countries. Don't worry, though, everything is going to be fine. All the men in Israel are going to fight back and drive away the people who attacked us and I am going to help them. I will take care of our soldiers who might get sick or hurt. I will come back home very soon. Mommy will stay at home and your aunt Zipi will also be here soon and they will both be with you."

My daughter Dafna seemed to take it all in stride and, as the oldest, seemed calm and unperturbed. She quietly and attentively listened to my explanation and nodded her head with understanding. I was amazed at her maturity and hoped that she truly understood and would remain unruffled, even if things became more difficult. My son, three year old Danny, kept playing quietly with his toy cars on the floor and did not seem to understand or be concerned about the situation. A short time after my wife returned from the grocery store, I hugged each of them and again bid them goodbye. When I closed the apartment door behind me I was not sure if I would ever see my wife and children again.

Chapter 5
The Drive South

We finally left the base at about one o'clock in the afternoon of October seventh. We headed south, forming a convoy that stretched like a long snake over several kilometers. Our van was one of the last vehicles to leave; as a result, we trailed the convoy. This was standard procedure so that in case of an emergency we could take care of any medical issues that arose. I sat by the driver, Avi; the medics were seated in the back. They looked both anxious and eager, as we faced the great unknown.

In the beginning we passed by the familiar sights of Kiryhat Malachi and Kiryat Gat, then Kibutz Nitzanim and Kibutz Yad Mordechay. Cultivated fields, orchards, and plowed fields lined both sides of the road. I could not help remembering that these last two settlements stopped the advance of the Egyptian Army during the War of Liberation in 1948. Even though both were eventually captured by the advancing army, the defense of these settlements by less than a hundred men and women bought Israel precious days for the defense of Tel Aviv. The valor and determination of the members of these settlements allowed the two week old nation to build up enough forces and repel the imminent threat to the survival of the country. Even though we were at a perilous period, I was somewhat relieved that the upcoming battle with the Egyptians would take place far away from the main population centers of the country. We traveled around the Gaza strip and after a few hours, reached the Sinai Desert. The cultivated green fields were gone and the sandy desert wasteland was all around us.

Our battalion had about 270 trucks, which included water and gasoline tankers as well as other heavy vehicles, and therefore moved slowly along the roads. We had to travel about 250 kilometers to reach the Suez Canal region and, as we entered the Sinai, the roads consisted of two-lane narrow strips. The way south was crowded with other military convoys heading to the front. It was difficult at times to follow our convoy because vehicles not part of our battalion often overtook our van, causing us to lose contact with our battalion's vehicles ahead of us. We had to maneuver on numerous occasions and overtake other vehicles to keep pace with our battalion. Oftentimes other convoys of troops, tanks, and artillery became intermingled with ours. Fortunately, we were able to maintain visual contact with our convoy because our battalion's trucks stood out among other vehicles. This was a challenging task and all of us helped our driver locate our convoy by spotting elements of our battalion on the road ahead of us.

For many hours a stream of advice and directions came from the passengers to our driver:

"You can pass this truck now, Avi. Don't hesitate; the road is clear!"

"Are you sure this is the right way?"

"Turn right in the intersection!"

"Bear to the left, there's a tank stuck on the shoulders of the road!"

After we crossed the old border of Israel into the Sinai Peninsula there were fewer side roads and intersections where we could get lost. In addition, personnel from our regiment were stationed at major junctions to instruct us how to proceed. Because our van, like many other vehicles, did not have a wireless communication system, our battalion's operational officer and his deputy kept driving back and forth on their jeeps conveying orders, delivering messages, and ensuring that vehicles were not lost. They did their best to create a communication system between the commanding officer and each vehicle. This was, however, a poor substitute to an internal wireless communication system within our battalion.

As the hours of driving dragged on the conversation we carried on was flowing:

"You need to speed up so that you can catch the tail of our convoy."

"We're going to stop here for a while."

"Now that night is falling, don't turn your head lights on and just use the parking lights."

"Doc, there's a driver with a terrible headache ahead of you. Can we get him some pain medication?

Portions of the roads had been damaged by tanks which had left deep marks on the asphalt. Apparently many of the tanks were not carried by tank-transporters, but traveled using their own tracks. The tanks roared by, generating clouds of dust mixed with black smoke, proving how desperate the situation was. Deep tank grooves on the pavement underscored the urgency of the tank crews as they sped forward toward their destination. Having the tanks reach the battlefield on their own is damaging to their engines and tracks as well as the roads. The fact that the army was having the tanks travel long distances on their own power, rather than by the faster and safer system of tank transporters, was another sign that we had been caught by surprise; there was probably no time to wait for the arrival of the more cumbersome transporters, which were undoubtedly in short supply.

Another indication of our desperate situation was the sight of so many tanks and other vehicles that had become stuck on the sides of the roads as they made their way south. Some likely had mechanical problems and many of the tanks exhibited broken tracks. Crews were working hard to replace the chains, hammering and pulling the broken tracks in the middle of the busy roads. Many seemed to be assisted by specialized mechanical repair units that were fixing broken engines. Some crew members sat idly by their tanks, apparently waiting for roadside assistance. I wondered how these tank crews would eventually meet up again with their units once they had repaired their vehicles.

The slow drive to the front was unnerving. We stopped frequently due to congestion on the roads as convoys of troops and tanks bypassed us. I kept asking myself again and again —*Why were we not called up earlier? We should have been at the front two or three days ago! Whose fault is this?* Apparently I was not the only one who asked these questions.

On occasion, our entire convoy stopped by the side of the road. We used those brief respites to get out of the van, stretch, and walk around. Avi used those stops to fill the van's tank with gasoline that he got from spare fuel containers. Our brief conversations were mostly about our military situation – we all speculated about what was going on:

"The Arabs took advantage of Yom Kippur to attack us. How could they have surprised us this way?"

"Why didn't our intelligence know about the attack ahead of time?"

"It's Golda's (Prime Minister Golda Meir) fault. She has no military knowledge or experience."

"No, it's Dayan who's to blame! He's too arrogant for his own good and way too friendly to the Arabs."

"They kicked Sharon out of the army and now we don't have a decent commander capable of repelling the Egyptians."

"Don't worry! We'll teach the Egyptians a lesson they'll never forget. We'll break them like we did in '56 in the Sinai Campaign and in '67 in the Six Day War. We just need another chance to teach their lesson!"

"What chutzpah! –Attacking us on Yom Kippur!"

The sense that the country's leadership had lost our trust was overwhelming. Throughout the long, frantic rush to the front, we continued to try to figure out what had brought us to this precipice, becoming increasingly depressed and disheartened.

We drove all day long and continued driving on after sunset throughout the night, constantly passing tank crews working on their broken vehicles, aided by flashlights or the headlights of other vehicles.

Avi, our driver, seemed to become increasingly more irritated and erratic in his driving. On one occasion he almost hit a truck ahead of us. He kept shouting at other drivers, obviously becoming more and more impatient. I looked at him and realized that he seemed to be very tired. Driving for so many hours and making so many unexpected stops must have been very demanding and exhausting. I suggested that he take a short rest while I replace him. He vehemently protested, asserting that he was not tired and quite able to continue. He also reminded me that, according to army regulations, he was the only one permitted to drive the van. I had to use my authority to convince him to let go of the steering wheel and explained that driving while being so worn out put us all in danger. I assured him that, as the officer in charge of the medical unit, I would assume the responsibility of ordering him to give up the steering wheel.

Once we switched places, Avi fell deeply asleep sitting up in the front seat. I drove for several hours until Avi woke up and we switched places again. Whenever he took over the steering wheel I napped. We kept switching roles like this all night long and throughout the following day. Even though we were all tired, the realization that we were at war kept us going. It seemed that the surge of adrenalin created by the situation made it easier to overcome our exhaustion.

I had only a general idea about our location; the small map of the Sinai Desert that I carried was my only reference. From the road, I recognized the tall date trees of the coastal town of El Arish. During our tour of the Sinai Desert with the Egged bus company a few months earlier, we had stopped to take pictures of the rows of these beautiful trees. We bought tasty dates from Bedouin youngsters who ran toward our tour bus offering their merchandise. Today, however, none of these children could be seen and the town's streets appeared desolate.

I realized that we were advancing south and west through the northern Sinai road which ran through El Arish. This was the shortest road to the Suez Canal and ran by the military base of Baluza. Our battalion's operational officer informed us of reports about Egyptian commandos who had been dropped behind our lines and that we needed to be ready for the possibility of an attack. Occasionally we heard the deep rumble of jets soaring overhead. I told Avi that I hoped that those planes were Israeli and not Egyptian. Preceded and followed by kilometers long lines of tanks, jeeps, and trucks, we were an enticing target for attacks from the air.

Chapter 6
Too Close to the Front

As we proceeded to the front and passed the town of Romani, I started to hear from far away the sounds of artillery shelling. It was not clear whose artillery I was hearing – ours or the Egyptians'. We finally halted at about eight in the evening after more than thirty-one hours of on and off driving; we were told that we would remain at that location overnight. I estimated that we were stationed about fifteen kilometers south of Baluza on the road leading to the military base of Tassa. Ahead of us on the left were open desert dunes surrounded by low lying hills. On the right, low sandy hills marked the horizon toward the Suez Canal. The sounds of artillery and explosions came from that direction.

Although it was night, it was not completely dark – the moon and stars shone brightly as they always did in the desert. I have always been amazed by the beauty of the stars in the Sinai. I remembered how much I enjoyed watching the sky at night whenever I spent time in Sinai for a reserve duty or as a tourist. I always searched for the familiar North Star, the Big and Small Dippers, the Cassiopeia, the Soldier Star Formations, and the Milky Way Galaxy. For an instant I forgot that we were in the desert during a war and that imminent danger surrounded us. The stars were more visible here than they were in the city, both an advantage and a handicap. We could clearly see the sand dunes and desert terrain all around us for almost a kilometer. So, however, could our adversaries; thus, the advantage of using the darkness to hide or operate clandestinely was lost.

Everyone was exhausted after of the long stop-and-go driving in heavy traffic. However, the sounds of artillery fire and the sense that we were not far from the battle kept us alert and focused. We were told to park our vehicles far apart from each other on a large sandy dune west of the hills shielding us from the canal, the scene of the fighting. Maintaining a distance of at least thirty meters between each vehicle would help prevent massive loss in case of attack.

As I considered our position, I was relieved to see that we were parked among the command and communication vehicles, while the trucks carrying ammunition and gasoline were parked further away. This was a wise precaution because of the danger posed should any of them be hit by enemy fire. Such potential danger actually felt very immediate, as the sounds of battle seemed to be quite close. Indeed, our deputy commanding officer told us of an imminent threat from Egyptian commandos who had landed by helicopter throughout the area, intent on attack. Although he could not give us more information about the exact location of these commandos, the sounds of the battle and the unfamiliar environment made the threat very real and ominous.

The sergeant major instructed me to organize my crew and supplies and to ensure that one of us would be on watch throughout the night. I arranged a watch roster and made sure that the rifles of all my medics were in good shape. Unfortunately, they were each issued the same old Czechoslovakian rifle that had been issued to most of our battalion. A reliable manual rifle, it was no match for any modern automatic weapon. Since we were a supply battalion and not a fighting unit, this was the best the military had to offer us. The result, however, was that we were extremely vulnerable to a commando attack. However, by that point, I was so tired and had so much work to do that I could not dwell on these worries.

We still had no idea what was going on, especially where the enemy was located. Some of the soldiers parked near us conveyed the latest rumors and these were not good. They described numerous casualties among our troops, missile attacks on our rear bases in Sinai, and widespread attacks by Egyptian commandos. The realization that even the furthest military bases in Sinai were vulnerable to missile attacks was hard to digest. Long range missiles had never before been used in any Middle East war and their introduction escalated the dangers and increased our vulnerability. It was especially painful to hear that women soldiers had been killed in these attacks. I had always felt protective of the women in our ranks and their deaths underscored for me the ineffectiveness of our defenses.

News from the Golan Heights, where our forces were desperately fighting a superior Syrian tank force, was no less ominous. Numerous Israeli planes had been downed by enemy missiles on both fronts. It seemed clear that only a small army of regular Israeli forces were on hand to challenge the surprise enemy attacks, as the reservists, the mainstay of the Israeli military, were at home observing Yom Kippur.

A short time after arriving at our rest stop we heard a radio announcement that the Chief of Staff of the Israeli Defense Forces, General David Elazar ("Dado") would be delivering a speech at nine p.m. We were very anxious to finally hear an official presentation about what had happened. Although I certainly hoped to hear some good or promising news, mostly I wanted to hear the truth. The Israeli military and the Israeli government had always prided themselves on being truthful and forthright about any situation. Arab countries often boasted about their victories, even when obviously losing, making their news reports inherently unbelievable. I expected Dado's delivery to be an accurate rendition of what had transpired, painful as it undoubtedly would be.

At precisely nine p.m. everyone gathered around their vehicles or next to those holding transistor radios. My medics and I huddled around our van and turned our radio to the highest volume. There was a tense expectation in the air. We were finally going to hear an official description of what had transpired earlier and what was going on throughout the battlefields.

47

The short speech described the sudden attack by Egypt and Syria and informed the public that Israeli forces were counterattacking and wining back lost territory. Dado reported that Israel tanks had reached the Suez Canal, concluding with the exhortation that "We will break the bones of our enemies." It was a bizarre ending to a speech that everyone had awaited. This was language that no Israeli leader had ever used before and, in fact, was eerily similar to the bombastic and unbelievable declarations of our foes. It felt like he was trying to achieve in words what he could not attain on the battle field. Judging by the rumbling of canons around us and the stories I had been hearing, it seemed that our own bones were the ones that were being broken. This was the first time in my life that I realized I could not trust the information delivered by our leaders. My faith in the veracity of the military and the government was shaken. This realization compounded the growing sensation that the war was not going well.

After hearing the speech I decided to make a visit to each of the four companies comprising our regiment: general supply, gasoline, ammunition, and water. I wanted to be able to attend to the medical needs of the soldiers at each company and thought that, even if there were no medical problems at that moment, it would be a good idea to show my presence; knowing that the regiment's physician was there for them would hopefully make the soldiers feel a bit more secure. Two of my medics, Shmuel and Avner, immediately agreed to join me, despite the fact that they were clearly exhausted. The other two stayed behind, napping in their sleeping bags on the sand close to our van.

Before leaving, I reminded our driver not to use the van's headlights so as not to alert the enemy of our position. Happily, visibility around us was quite good. Navigating in our van-ambulance to all four companies, we completed our tour within an hour, speaking to each of the company's commanders and encountering only minor medical problems. Most of the soldiers were exhausted after the long drive, yet their apprehension and anxiety were evident. As I drove around, I could not ignore the realization that, as a supply battalion carrying ammunition and gasoline and without any firepower to defend ourselves, we were an easy target for enemy attack.

As it turned out, we were parked only a short distance from the Division's Medical Support Battalion, an advanced medical unit carrying sophisticated equipment and comprehensive medical supplies, as well as a field hospital. Since we needed several essential medical supplies, I ignored the late hour and decided to pay the medical battalion a visit on the way back. We arrived at a group of large tents forming a field hospital that reminding me of the movie "Mash." The desert sky was dark but the hospital had its own electric generator and was therefore dimly lit. To my astonishment, the atmosphere was festive and upbeat, not unlike the ambiance of the movie.

Although they were not yet taking care of wounded soldiers, the medical team was busy setting up the post. At eleven o'clock at night the place swarmed with medics, nurses, physicians, and other personnel installing, inspecting, and cataloguing their medical and surgical equipment. Surprisingly, the people I met appeared to be in high spirits. In fact, after one of the physicians learned that I was the medical officer for the supply battalion, he jokingly asked why I hadn't brought them any fresh cakes or other desserts. Brief discussions, however, revealed that beneath the jovial attitude there was general worry and apprehension. Some of officers confirmed the rumors I had heard earlier about the dire situation of our military, one noting that we had suffered many casualties and had made no military gains: "There is just a lot of confusion everywhere."

I recognized three of my medical school classmates whom I had not seen since we graduated six years earlier. They had been called up, as I had been, two days earlier. Two had been doing residencies in surgery and the other was specializing in internal medicine.

Avraham, a surgical resident, was tall and skinny. He had served as an officer in the paratrooper corps prior to medical school and was a captain in the Medical Corps. He welcomed me warmly, jokingly asserting that he was going to organize a reunion of our class in Cairo next week.

Avraham beamed with an aura of self confidence that projected the impression that he could handle any situation that may arise. However, after talking to him for a few minutes, I realized that he was also concerned about being so close to the front without any tactical support. He was especially apprehensive about his medics not having any protection except for their personal weapons. He felt that the medical battalion was situated too close to the fighting where it could be hit by direct enemy fire or even be overrun by enemy troops. He was also worried about being attacked by Egyptian commandos that might have landed in the vicinity. We both suspected that in the confusion and rush to move forward, our support battalions were placed too close to the front.

The information I received from my friends at the Medical Support Battalion strengthened my growing suspicion that we were at risk of suffering casualties and losing our supplies should we encounter combat. As a supply regiment, our tactical position should have been at a safe distance behind the fighting forces. We were the "soft belly" of the tanks division, essential for its operation but vulnerable to attack.

Avraham and my other classmates were willing to give me the medical supplies I requested, but asked me a favor in return. Realizing that I was the physician for the supply battalion, they asked me to bring them a box of hand grenades that might become useful in case they were attacked by enemy troops or commandos. They had served as regular soldiers during their obligatory service and were trained for battle. They felt, nevertheless, that they would need additional supplies to meet this anticipated challenge.

It was an unusual request and I was surprised to hear it, although, upon reflection, it did not seem illogical. Feeling my friends' genuine distress and sensing their actual danger, I promised that I would do my best and get to it right away. I did not want to disappoint my friends and felt good about being able to provide them with potentially life-saving supplies. However, I could not escape sensing the paradox I faced. I was asking them to provide me with medical supplies to save lives and, in return, my friends were asking me for supplies to end lives. The irony of supplying hand grenades to physicians so that they could remain alive to care for the injured seemed emblematic of the dire situation confronting us.

We drove back to the ammunition company, hoping to get our hands on a case of hand grenades. I was able to locate Major Stern to whom I had spoken an hour earlier when I visited his company. I had known Stern since we were both three years old because our fathers played soccer together on Hapoel Haifa teams. Our fathers, in turn, had known each other since 1931 when they played together on the famous Jewish soccer team, HaKoach Vienna, in Austria. As teammates, they had immigrated to Palestine in 1934. Stern and I had not seen each other for almost thirty years; we were surprised and happy to meet again when we were both assigned to the same reserve supply battalion.

Stern was surprised to see me again at that late hour and even more surprised when I told him why I had returned. Although he was willing to help my colleagues, he had a problem. He could not easily retrieve a single box of hand grenades because they were all placed inside large containers holding over thirty boxes each. The containers, in turn, were inside huge ammunition trucks. We went over to one of the a trucks and I waited as Stern climbed on top and attempted to open one of the containers with a crow bar. It was a strange site to see Major Stern standing on top of an ammunition supply truck at midnight searching for a hand grenades box to hand over to a friend. After some time he was finally able to open one of the containers and carefully extracted a box of fifty hand grenades. He dismounted the truck and delivered the cherished box to me.

When we returned to the Medical Support Battalion the place was still full of activity. My friends were elated upon seeing the hand grenades that we delivered. *How tragic, I thought, that physicians need a supply of hand grenades to be able to perform their job with less fear.* I kept two hand grenades for myself, just in case, cautiously placing them in a pouch attached to my belt along with an extra cartridge of bullets for my Uzi. I fervently hoped that I would never need them. Ever since the time that I had seen the devastating damage they can inflict, I treated hand grenades very cautiously. It was in medical school, during my two week rotation in forensic medicine, when I saw a soldier who had been mortally wounded when the hand grenade he carried on his belt exploded unexpectedly. The sight of his injuries was unforgettable. We drove back to our battalion with the extra medical supplies we had obtained, as well as a box of canned fruit from my friends as a show of gratitude.

I finally got a few hours of sleep inside the van, frequently interrupted by noises of explosions and moving trucks. I was so tired after the previous sleepless night that I fell asleep right away. Early in the morning the battalion's messenger came rushing over and delivered a hurried order:

"Get moving! Now that it's daylight we can't stay here! We're going to move backwards by driving eastward."

"What is going on? Why do we have to retreat, and what's the rush?" I wondered.

"We're too close to the front line and in danger of being hit by enemy fire or even overrun by Egyptian tanks."

The constant explosions confirmed my previous suspicions and apprehensions. The noise seemed louder and closer than it had been the night before. I assumed that the confusion and rush to arrive at the front contributed to the error of stationing us too close to the fighting.

We quickly commenced our retreat to a safer location. We drove by the Medical Support Battalion which was also in the process of unfolding its field hospital. I was happy to hear that they had had an uneventful night and had not needed to use the hand grenades.

We stopped approximately fifteen kilometers east, where the sounds of battle were harder to hear. Our battalion parked its vehicles along a stretch of desert roads and waited. Although we changed our position several times in the ensuing days, we essentially remained at a safe distance from the front, staying east of the lateral road that ran from the Baluza to the Tassa military bases.

Soon after our move an order came from the Israeli Military Central Command that all women soldiers were to vacate the Sinai Peninsula battle zone. It was a surprising order and illustrated how dire our situation had become. I assumed that the order was given because of the sensitivity of the Israeli public to losing female soldiers in battle. Women were never assigned to fighting units, but once it became clear that the war would not be restricted to the front, they were at risk everywhere.

As I saw the young women huddled on a truck and waving goodbye, I had mixed feelings about their departure. On the one hand, I was sorry to see them leave because they were an essential element of our resources and balanced the predominance of males in our battalion. Their presence also lifted the morale of the men. On the other hand, I was relieved that we would no longer have to worry about their safety. Since there was always a risk of becoming a prisoner of war, I worried that women were at risk of being abused and tortured. As their truck disappeared down the road to the rear, I told myself, *This is now going to be a war between 'Men Only'.*

Chapter 7
The Price of War

As we settled by the roadside on the morning of October nine, I established a daily routine, similar to what we had done during our previous battalion's maneuvers. We had daily sick calls, made regular trips to all the companies in the battalion, and formed a nightly watch around our van. The tankers and trucks in our battalion began to make repeated trips to the front lines to supply the fighting forces with ammunition, gas, food, and water. We still had very limited information about what was actually transpiring on the front, and I understood for the first time what "Battle Fog" actually means. Most of the information we received was from news heard over the radio. I did get some glimpses of what was happening from talking to soldiers who came to sick call after returning from the front and when I made my daily trips to the various companies in the battalion.

The first person to tell me about the events on the front was a truck driver who came to sick call because of a bruised right elbow. He looked tired and his lean face was unshaven and covered with desert dust. I noted that his hands were stained with black tar and grease. After washing the dirt from his elbow, I noticed that he had a serious burn on his right hand. Puzzled, I asked him how he had sustained his injury.

"I was unloading ammunition boxes from my truck onto an armored troop carrier not far away from the fighting. We were very close to the battle line and I was rushing to finish as soon as possible and get out of the area. Suddenly I saw one of our tanks burst into flames from a direct missile hit. Two crew members jumped out; I guess the others did not survive. One of the soldiers was on fire. I ran to him and tried to put the flames out. The other crew member helped me, but we had a lot of difficulty; the poor man was screaming in agony. Finally, we were able to stanch the fire after covering the soldier with a blanket and rolling him in it. I must have sustained these burns and bruises then."

While this story was certainly shocking, the most disconcerting aspect of the account was the dispassionate and matter-of-fact manner in which the soldier relayed his experience. It seemed that he had already become resigned to the risks of battle.

"What happened to the rest of the tank crew?" I asked.

"We tried to get to them out of the burning tank, but the fire was too intense. We were afraid that the ammunition inside the tank would explode at any minute and I had to retreat immediately because of the intense fighting that was going on. I was afraid my truck would be also hit and that all the ammunition on it would explode, killing everyone around us."

"And what did you do then?" I inquired.

"I ran off and waited about three hundred meters away until things quieted down; then I returned to finish my job."

I asked Ehud to clean the man's wound and place a bandage over it. His injuries were not serious and he did not need to be evacuated. I was concerned, however, that he would not be able to keep his wounds clean or drive his truck with a bandaged arm.

He brushed off my concerns, telling me "Doc, I can drive my truck with one hand if necessary. Don't worry – I'm a seasoned driver. Besides, I'm really needed."

"At least come back every couple of days so that we can change your bandages and make sure that the wounds are healing," I advised.

"I promise," he replied, got back on his truck and drove away. I looked for him whenever I made my daily drive to his company but he was apparently always away, bringing ammunition to the tanks on the front. I never saw him again.

Other drivers came back with harrowing stories about the failed Israeli efforts to repel the Egyptian forces back across the canal and our forces' futile attempts to recapture the ten to fifteen kilometer long stretch of land the Egyptians had seized along the Suez Canal. The soldiers also described the numerous casualties our forces had suffered and how many of the powerful Israeli tanks were set ablaze by the Egyptians. Apparently the Egyptians were using a new and unrecognized method - a hand - held antitank missile launcher that was able to fire a guided missile. This weapon was used by infantry stationed at a safe distance; when the missile hit a tank it often penetrated its armor and killed or wounded everyone inside. The soldiers recounted their despair as they witnessed the demolition of tanks that had been hit by a missile. Some described in great detail the damage inside the tanks and the extent of the crew members' injuries. I was told that many tank battalions had been assigned an additional medical team, including a physician, because of the high casualty rates and the severity of injuries. Two physicians for each tank battalion were probably needed to care for the injured and save as many as possible. It was becoming clear to me that the philosophy of the medical corps – bring medical care as close as possible to the injured – was being implemented.

I personally saw the devastating effects of these missiles. On the afternoon of October 10, we received an urgent message that two of our soldiers had been hurt in a car accident. We took our van and drove westward, looking for the accident site. After driving for about seven kilometers, we came to a derailed water tanker lying on its side. Several other vehicles had already arrived and the driver and his passenger had been extracted and placed on the side of the road. I could hear the sounds of heavy artillery not far away and observed several of our tanks stationed on the hills south of us. Since each tank had a wireless radio, I assumed that one of these tank crews had informed our battalion about the derailed truck.

After a quick assessment, I diagnosed that the driver had fractured his left foot, while his passenger had only minor facial injuries from broken glass. I stabilized the driver's broken leg on a supporting piece of wood using bandages, administered morphine, and started an intravenous infusion. We placed both wounded men in our van and headed toward the Baluza military base, about twelve kilometers away and overlooking the Suez Canal. We then headed toward the field hospital where we delivered the wounded soldiers for further treatment.

The emergency treatment area was in a big tent and was very crowded. The medical staff, caring for at least a dozen wounded soldiers, moved frantically among the patients. Most patients seemed to be stable but several required artificial ventilation. Behind the array of tubes, drainage catheters, infusion lines, and oxygen masks, I could barely see the charred faces of the wounded. Despite the frantic activity, the place was relatively quiet and seemed to be running very efficiently. I realized that I had delivered the two wounded men at a time the hospital was being overburdened by an influx of patients.

"We just got a truckload of wounded soldiers from the front; they all have burns and shrapnel wounds," the head medic told me." We've been working non-stop for the past four days, and the influx of injured men doesn't seem to end."

Even thought the piece of paper listing the medications given to the wounded was attached to their shirts, I explained the injuries of our soldiers to one of the physicians and made sure that he knew which medications they had been given.

In one corner of the tent I noticed that one wounded soldier's uniform was different from those of the rest. As I approached him, I quickly realized that he was an Egyptian soldier. Next to him, sat an armed Israeli soldier keeping watch. The Egyptian was a mustached, dark skinned man in his thirties. He seemed to be huge; the hospital stretcher could barely contain his muscular frame. Looking at him, I thought he would be a formidable foe in battle. His chest and face were bandaged and he was receiving intravenous infusion and oxygen through a tracheostomy. I looked at his face and sensed fear in his eyes. I wondered if he was terrified of us or if he appeared so frightened because his wounds were very serious.

"This is an Egyptian commando soldier captured after being seriously wounded in the chest. He also sustained a bullet injury in the face and was bleeding very heavily from his mouth. We had to perform an emergency tracheostomy on him to enable him to breathe. He's doing much better now and is to be transported to a rear field hospital on the next helicopter flight." The head medic gave me this background, as I stared at the wounded commando.

It was strange to actually face our adversary. On the one hand, I resented him because of what he and his fellow soldiers were doing to our soldiers. On the other, I was proud that he was being cared for in the same way as our own soldiers were being treated and by the very same medical team. I fervently hoped that our captured wounded were being given the same level of care.

On the advice of the soldiers guarding the main gate of the base, I decided to take a shortcut through side roads toward the site of our battalion. The road was quiet, with very little traffic. It was unnerving to be driving in unfamiliar territory and I was worried that we might be heading in the wrong direction since we had no maps to guide us and my personal tour map of Sinai did not show the road we were on. After about fifteen minutes I noted a solitary Israeli tank approximately fifty meters off the road. As we came closer, I realized that the Patton tank was deserted. Strange, I thought. Although its body tilted slightly to the side, the tank looked intact. I dismounted the van and, as I walked toward the tank, I observed a small hole below its turret. This tiny hole, where the missile had apparently penetrated the armor, was the only sign that the tank had been hit, probably a few hours earlier. It had been left as a lonely sentry, most likely destined to be towed away later.

When I climbed to the turret and looked into the tank I found its inside completely destroyed. The smell of the burning interior was very strong and I could sense the odor of scorched human flesh mixed with that of burnt fuel. I could only imagine what had happened to the crew and hoped that at least some of them had survived.

I was shaken by this experience. Tanks were a symbol of Israel's military might; the country had always prided itself in having a superlative tank corps capable of winning any battle. Such was the experience in the Six Day War that had taken place only six years earlier. This invincibility was evident during the Independence Day parade that celebrated Israel's 25th anniversary only five months earlier. I had traveled to Jerusalem with a friend to watch the parade. Sitting in the viewing stands under the ancient walls of the Old City, we felt the ground shaking as the tanks rumbled by. They seemed so mighty and I felt both proud of my country and secure for myself as I saw them drive by. Now I saw a similar tank lying incapacitated in the desert with a small hole in it, like a giant killed by a tiny pebble. To see this powerful machine destroyed by what must have been a mere foot soldier dissipated the lingering feeling of pride from the parade.

How could this happen? Why were we not ready for this type of missile? Why were we not informed about this weapon?

I had first heard about these deadly missiles only a couple of days earlier from radio reports, as well as from my fellow soldiers. The fact that everyone seemed to be surprised to hear of their existence in the battle field confirmed my sense that a small and vulnerable country like Israel could not afford this lack of intelligence. I had no answers to the questions that went through my mind at that moment. Again, I was confronted by the failure of the defense establishment to be prepared to deal with a new threat. I could only feel pain and anguish thinking about the men who had lost their lives inside the armor that was supposed to shield them. Surely they were very well trained tank corps crews who knew how to defend themselves and how to destroy other tanks. Yet they had no knowledge or training how to protect themselves from a lone infantryman carrying a missile.

I returned to the field hospital in Baluza the next day, this time to evacuate a soldier who had become dehydrated because of severe diarrhea. I had already recognized several of the personnel there and this time the transfer of our patient was smother and quicker. The place had become more chaotic than the day before and there were even a higher number of casualties present. I instinctively wanted to join the staff and help out in the hospital, but I felt that they did not really need me and realized that I needed to leave the emergency area as soon as possible so as not to interfere with the ongoing effort to salvage lives. Furthermore, I had my battalion to care for and needed to return as soon as possible. I was unable to know what was transpiring with the battalion because we lacked any radio communication.

As I stepped out of the tented area of the hospital and walked toward our van I saw nine stretchers lined up in a corner. I was stunned. These were our dead soldiers covered with blankets. I was not mentally prepared for this. These were the bodies of fallen Israelis who had paid the ultimate price. The sheer number of casualties was shocking. There were so many of them. Seeing the row of covered stretchers brought home the cost of this war. It struck me to see the steep price we were paying to survive and win this war. I immediately experienced the painful sense that I had lost someone close, like members of my own family. I had always felt that kind of pain when I learned about the death of an Israeli soldier or an Israeli citizen, especially someone who had died prematurely. I had always retained the feeling that every Jew is a close relative. Growing up in a small country, surrounded by enemies, made me feel as though we had been weakened by the death of any one of us.

Although I had previously witnessed our war casualties, especially during the Six Day War, I felt different this time, perhaps because I had become a father and now had a family of my own. Moreover, over the years, I had experienced the loss in battle of several close friends and had seen the devastating effects of their deaths on their families. *These dead soldiers must have families and friends who are worried about them and who are waiting and praying for their return. They do not know yet that their loved ones are dead. They are still hoping that they are okay.* I shivered when I thought about the impending visit by the military authorities to the soldiers' families and of their sorrow and pain as they learn about the death of their family members. It dawned on me that not only are the soldiers the victims; it is also their wives, children, parents, grandparents and friends that will be forever traumatized. Their lives will be eternally changed. I had never gotten over this realization and never will.

I braced myself to keep what I had experienced from affecting me. I told myself that I had to get used to living with these realities and to not allow these thoughts and feelings from interfering with my immediate task: caring for the wellbeing of those under my care and preventing, as much as possible, death and injury. I bore my pain and drove off in the van.

Chapter 8
Waiting in the Desert

I had always made sure that I carried my Uzi and wore my helmet at all times to set an example for the reserve soldiers who were often lax in maintaining their military demeanor. I realized that others were looking up to me and that I had the responsibility to show them the need to carry the right equipment in the event of sudden danger. Although I was often personally lax about military demeanor (never paying great attention to my uniform or the proper method of saluting), I realized that these basic matters were essential for survival; it was up to me to set an example to others. During maneuvers and training, I was the least enthusiastic of my colleagues about military protocol, but during war time I needed to be a role model. Like most soldiers, I did not shave on a daily basis because of the need to conserve water, and I rarely had the opportunity to take a shower or do my laundry. However, these were less important in my eyes than being able to protect the lives of our soldiers.

I started to conduct a daily sick call for my battalion at noon but did not turn away anyone who came with an urgent problem at any other time. This was the routine we used during our previous maneuvers, and the battalion's soldiers were aware of and used to this practice. I conducted the sick call at the back of our van which was parked on the side of the road. It was difficult to allow for privacy in that setting, but I could close the doors of the van in case I needed to perform a thorough examination. Surprisingly, very few soldiers came to see me with routine medical problems and only a handful requested to be sent back home because of their medical condition. This was far different from my previous experience during routine maneuvers and training exercises. What appeared to be responsible for this change in attitude was the current state of war. I assumed that everyone felt, as I did, that this war was for the survival of our country and thus minor medical problems could be easily disregarded.

Right after sunset one evening we heard an alarm for incoming fire. Together with my medics, I crouched in the ditch beside the road as gunfire sounded in the distance. Suddenly, a middle aged soldier and a sergeant approached us. My first thought was that someone had been hit in the barrage. Instead, they joined us in the ditch and the soldier explained why he had come to see me.

"My captain sent me to see you because he wanted you to relieve me of my duties so that I can leave the front," he calmly stated. It was late in the evening and I could barely see his face. I was, however, able to observe his serious demeanor and dispassionate voice.

"I miraculously survived twice when my truck was hit by enemy fire and later burned as I was delivering gasoline to the tanks in the front. I think my luck has run out – if this happens again, I won't survive." He said calmly.

The sergeant accompanying him nodded his head, confirming that the soldier's incredible story was indeed true.

Even though the man described a terrifying experience, he was without emotion, and spoke calmly and logically. There was clearly a dichotomy between his terrifying description and his impassive presentation. It seemed that whatever he had experienced had not affected him in a visible way.

This was an unusual request. Something did not seem right in the way he presented himself because there was a contrast between what he told me and how he looked and behaved. He was neither distressed nor upset. This seemed strange, considering what he had apparently been through. I thought carefully about the situation and could not find any medical reason to dismiss him. On the other hand, he had described a frightening and harrowing experience that might have affected him deeply in ways that I could not see.

I thought for a minute and told him:

"I understand that your commander feels that you should leave. Since there's no visible medical reason that I can find to justify your discharge, he should be the one who decides about letting you go."

The soldier did not protest and again showed no emotion. He calmly accepted my decision and left. I was unsure whether I had made the right decision. The soldier most probably needed to be let go so that he could recuperate from his near death experiences. However, I felt that the reason for sending him back should be administrative and not medical. My main concern was not to allow commanders to manipulate me into relieving their soldiers without a medical cause and to use the route of a medical discharge for non-medical reasons. It seemed to me that the soldier's commander did not understand my role as a physician who could make decisions only with respect to medical and psychological issues. I learned later that the soldier's commander had decided to let him leave the following morning.

An unusual complaint during a routine sick call examination led me to prevent a major medical problem in the fighting units. It happened on the fifth day of the war when we were parked along the side of the road about fifteen kilometers from the front.

It was a warm and windy day and I had just finished a routine sick call that had lasted about two hours. I had seen about half a dozen soldiers who had a variety of minor medical problems including allergy, cough, and muscle strain. At about two in the afternoon, as we were winding down the clinic and placing our medical equipment back in the boxes, two soldiers from the ammunition company came to see me. They apologized for not coming earlier, reporting that they had felt fine until about an hour before, when they began to experience vomiting, abdominal pain, and diarrhea. Although they appeared to be in good health, they described a lot of discomfort.

My first question was to try and ascertain the source of their illness.

"Did you eat or drink anything that might have given you an upset stomach?" I asked.

"No, we had nothing unusual to eat, but the water we drank two hours ago tasted bad and had a strange smell."

"Do you have any of this water with you?" I asked.

"Yes, I have some left over in my canteen," one of them answered.

I asked him to give me his canteen. When I unscrewed the cap I smelled an intense odor of gasoline. It was clear to me that the water he drank was tainted with gasoline and that this was the cause of the symptoms he and his colleague had described. It was a serious situation if drinking water had become contaminated, especially in the desert where every drop of water was precious.

"Where did you get the water from?" I immediately inquired.

"We got it from a small mobile water tanker brought to us a few hours ago."

I immediately realized that I was facing an urgent problem that could have a devastating effect on many more individuals - contamination of drinking water with gasoline. I had to act quickly to prevent others from becoming seriously ill.

"Show me where the water tanker is located," I demanded.

We boarded our van and drove about a kilometer down the road, guided by the two soldiers, until we arrived at the ammunition company. The water source was a large camouflaged tanker that had been towed to that location by a pickup truck. I climbed on top of the tanker and lifted its cover, instantly taken aback by a strong stench of gasoline. The water was definitely contaminated. I feared that we were facing a risky situation that could have endangered many more people and had to act quickly to prevent other soldiers from drinking the water and getting sick. I told the driver of the pickup truck about my discovery and asked him where he had filled up his tanker. He reported that he had filled it with water about three hours earlier from a large water tanker down the road. I told him to get into our van and help us locate that tanker knowing that I had to identify this source as soon as possible. Before leaving, I informed the officer in charge of the unit to make sure that no one else drank from the contaminated tanker.

Within a few minutes we arrived at the end of a convoy of six water tanker trucks. The engines of these trucks were running, as they were about to depart westward to supply the fighting forces with water. The truck drivers were already in their seats, waiting for the lead vehicle to start moving. I felt fortunate to have caught the trucks at the last minute before they left. I ordered the leading truck not to move and quickly scanned the trucks for any distinguishing signs that would help to identify the truck with tainted water. The water tankers, all in camouflage paint, looked identical to each other and were also indistinguishable from gasoline tankers, except for the designation "water" in small letters on their sides. Within seconds, I noticed that one of the six trucks was marked by a "gasoline" designation.

This was it! I had discovered the source of the water contamination. I climbed to the top of the tanker, opened its cap, and was struck by a strong stench of gasoline. The mystery was solved! In speaking with the officer in charge of the trucks I learned what must have happened. Someone had erroneously filled a gasoline tanker with water while the tankers were being filled up about twenty kilometers east of us from a large water pipe which brought water to the Sinai Peninsula from Israel. I wondered how such an error could have happened since the tanker had been clearly marked with a "gasoline" designation. This dangerous vehicle was about to be sent to quench the thirst of hundreds of soldiers in the midst of the fighting.

I had seen the water refilling pipe site during our maneuvers ten months earlier and I remembered how happy we were to have made this accidental discovery. We had run out of drinking water and were able to fill our canteens from the huge pipe. We were also happy to find this source of water because we were finally able to take showers after having been in the desert for more than a week. I remember how we stood naked under the huge faucet, letting the strong stream of water wash away the desert dust, indifferent to the fact that we were clearly visible on the side of the road. Having lived in the desert for many days, our standard of decency had clearly shifted!

It was apparent that the residue of gasoline which had floated to the top of the water in the tanker had caused the abdominal pain and diarrhea in the two soldiers I had seen earlier. I immediately ordered the tanker to be removed from the convoy. And, instead of ordering that the water be discarded, I suggested that it be used for showers by the men. I could only imagine what could have been the consequence of thirsty tank crews drinking gasoline- tainted water during a battle. In the midst of fighting, it would have been difficult for anyone to sense that they had been consuming tainted water. Abdominal pain and diarrhea could have incapacitated them and made it difficult to operate their tanks and other equipment. In my mind, I could see that the tainted water could have started a chain reaction that would have ended with my fellow soldiers becoming vulnerable to the enemy. I felt great relief and satisfaction having been able to solve this mystery, using my "detective" skills, in less than an hour. I realized that, in addition to being a battlefield doctor, I also needed to be an epidemiologist in order to safeguard the health of our troops.

Although I conducted a daily sick call, I also decided to tour the regiment's four companies every morning. I thought that by visiting on a daily basis I would be more available to the soldiers. These daily visits were very helpful to the soldiers because many would have not seen me if I would not have shown up in person. This was partially due to the fact that our battalion had to change locations every other day and also because the soldiers were busy with duties that often demanded long drives. During these visits to the troops I got to know more of the men and realized that most of those who came to see me just wanted to chat a little.

The daily trips turned out to be fairly risky, especially during early morning hours. Egyptian commandos were being dropped from helicopters throughout the desert during the night; their mission was to disrupt and destroy Israeli convoys. We had no idea if and where the Egyptians had been deployed and, accordingly, we were always at a state of alertness in case they should attack. We would occasionally hear and sometimes even see these helicopters pass over us. One night we saw three of them fly eastward a few kilometers south of us. Even though it was nighttime, we could spot the helicopters because they each had a single light that identified their positions. I was worried that they were planning to land near us and deliver their deadly human contents to attack our troops.

To our great relief, within a minute of the appearance of the helicopters, we heard heavy machine gun fire erupting from the hills directed at the choppers. I saw tracer bullets as these machine guns were illuminating the skies. The bullets found their targets; the three helicopters were hit – one after the other – and exploded in the air. Because of the darkness, I could not see if they fell to the ground immediately or completely disintegrated in the sky. Everyone around me cheered as we observed the exploding helicopters. Although I felt relief at the elimination of the danger, I also felt pity for the Egyptians soldiers inside these aircrafts as I imagined the inferno of their aircraft. Seeing the wounded Egyptian commando soldier at the field hospital in Baluza a day earlier made the enemy more human. It was a very unsettling feeling to know that the lives of so many human beings had ended in an instant in front of our eyes.

I instinctively thought about driving to the locations where the helicopters had fallen, just in case there were any survivors, but decided against it. I was deterred by the darkness and also because our van, not being equipped with four wheel drive, was not fit to drive on the soft sand. In the morning a reconnaissance unit investigating the crash sites found no survivors.

I was apprehensive each morning before taking the fifteen kilometer drive to visit our widely spread battalion. Accompanied by one of the medics and our driver, I had no idea what was awaiting us behind the many curves along the desolated desert roads. Before leaving, I loaded my weapon with a cartridge of bullets and placed my two hand grenades on the seat next to me. I rolled down my window and stuck my Uzi sub machinegun out in a "ready to fire" position and told the driver to proceed. I felt capable of handling an attack should it come, but was tense before every road curve and relieved after we had passed it or when another car came toward us from the opposite direction. It was reassuring to know that someone else had passed safely, meaning that the road ahead was safe. We did not converse much during these trips, as we were anxiously watching the road ahead. These tense trips took their toll on Avi, our driver, as well as on my medics, and I felt their anxiety all through our trips, especially when we saw no one around us. To reduce their exposures, I alternated the medics who accompanied me.

I knew that I would return fire to anyone who might attempt an attack on our vehicle. Yet I also was sure that, once the shooting would be over, I would care for anyone we might have wounded. This was a strange dichotomy: recognizing that we may need to kill in order to stay alive and then realizing that we would be caring for anyone we had tried to eliminate minutes earlier. Fortunately, we did not encounter any ambushes on our daily rounds.

The daily visits to each of the companies were very helpful and I felt that the risks of making these trips were worth it. The troops were expecting us and would wave us down in case they had a request or a medical problem. Some would just stop me to talk a little about what they had experienced the day before. I felt that such contact allowed some soldiers to vent some of their frustrations or ask for advice. In many cases I was able to avert simple medical problems before they had a chance to develop into major ones. These trips also enabled me to obtain firsthand information about the situation on the battlefield. As it was turning out, the truck drivers who made daily trips to the front to supply the tank brigades were the most informed in our battalion.

Chapter 9
Aerial Attacks

It was about two o'clock in the afternoon of October 11, the fifth day of the War, when we were suddenly attacked by two Egyptian MiG 19 jet fighters. We were just finishing our daily sick call and were caring for the last patient. I remember that he had elevated blood pressure and that I had prescribed some pills to deal with the problem. I was attempting to comfort him, explaining that his elevated blood pressure might have well been due to the tension we were all experiencing; I reassured him that his blood pressure would very likely decrease when the war ended. Suddenly, the unexpected occurred – we were being attacked from the air. A pair of Egyptian jet fighters emerged from behind the hills to the west and swooped down, spraying our trucks with machine gun fire. We were completely unprepared for an aerial assault and thus were taken by complete surprise. No one had warned us about the possibility of aerial attacks even though they should certainly have been expected. This was the first time that we had been attacked directly and it dawned on me that, although we were stationed at a safe distance behind the front, we would not be spared from attacks from the air.

I saw the planes before I could hear them as they were flying faster than the speed of sound. However, they came down so fast that we were all caught off guard. It was hard to see the planes with the sun in our eyes, but I could spot the shining silver metal of the jets' wings and could even observe the outline of the pilots in their cockpits as they flew only fifty meters above us. Machine gun fire was coming from underneath the wings as the aircraft rapidly approached. Only a second or two after the jets had passed over us did we hear their roaring engines.

Bullets struck the sand dunes north of the road, missing us by about thirty meters, and thus sparing us and the other vehicles from the assault. I could see the progressive strafing of the ground which created small holes in the sand and clouds of dust rising above them. It reminded me of scenes from war movies about the Battle of El-Alamein during the Second World War in Egypt. I had always been interested in that battle, fought in 1942, the year after I was born. Should the Germans have won that battle, they would have surely annihilated the Jewish inhabitants of Palestine just as they had done with the Jews in Europe.

Once the planes had flown over our position, I knew that we were safe for the moment, since a plane that had passed its target could not pose an immediate danger during that dive. It seemed that the jets had initially missed inflicting any damage, but I could see them circling on the horizon as they prepared to return for a second attack. It flashed in my mind: *We have less than a minute to do something to protect ourselves.* I remembered that an Israeli air force pilot had taught us during our medical officer's course that the best thing to do when being attacked by airplanes is to shoot back at them. Although the chance of hitting a fast flying jet with regular rifles is miniscule, the pilots, upon seeing the flares from weapons on the ground, become distracted and are prevented from fully concentrating on their targets.

Although we had no heavy weapons, I shouted at the soldiers around me to open fire as the jets approached us for their second and third sorties. Most of the men took cover under their trucks or the ditches around us, but some opened fire at the approaching jets with their single shot rifles – albeit without hitting any planes. I did not even consider firing my Uzi submachine gun, always on my shoulder, since its effective range was only a hundred meters – clearly useless against a jet. Fortunately, the jets missed their mark again and again, discharging a couple of bombs about a hundred meters from the road. As the jets were making their third bombing dive I heard a loud explosion after they had passed us. When I turned my head toward the sound, I observed a large burst of fire and smoke about a kilometer away.

Was anyone hurt? Was an ammunition truck or fuel tanker hit?

I was very concerned that the MiGs had hit one of the highly inflammable trucks of our battalion. Because our battalion was transporting highly inflammable materials, we were very susceptible to aerial attacks. My instinct was to drive immediately to the site of the explosion, but I decided to stay put just in case there were injuries among our own personnel. I watched the skies and saw that the jets turned west and disappeared over the horizon. Even though the whole incident lasted only several minutes it seemed as though it was hours.

Within a few minutes we received a message from the master sergeant who reported that the MiG's bombs had hit a collection of cooking gas containers lying on the sand. Two of our soldiers were slightly injured in their legs and would be brought over shortly. The gas tanks continued to explode for a while, generating a fire that burned for about an hour. Considering the potential devastation that could have been inflicted upon our defenseless column of vehicles, the actual damage was miniscule. I assumed that our battalion could live with less cooking gas.

Within fifteen minutes the two wounded soldiers were brought to me for treatment. They had suffered limited second degree burns in their legs. We tended to their injuries by giving them narcotics for the pain, cleaning the burned areas and bandaging their legs. I put them back in their jeep and evacuated them to the Baluza Military Base, about fifteen kilometers away, accompanied by our medic, Zvika. I didn't want to evacuate them in our van in order to keep all our medical equipment together and to preserve our mobility in the event of another aerial attack. Luckily, such an attack did not materialize, but we were all shaken by this incident.

How could it be that the Egyptian air force had acted with such impunity? This force hadn't played any role in the Six Day War when most of it had been decimated while still on the ground by a surprise Israeli attack on the first day of the war. We always believed in Israeli air force superiority but this time there was not one Israeli jet visible. We learned through rumors that numerous Israeli jets had been lost in the first forty-eight hours of the war, mostly by enemy surface to - air SAM missiles. We also realized that the overriding air force effort at that time was to assist in repelling the Syrian army, which was attempting to invade Israel after it had recaptured most of the Golan Heights. I assumed that whatever was left of the air force had been allocated to the northern front, thus leaving us without an aerial umbrella. As a result, it was left to us to defend ourselves on our own.

What also surprised me was that our battalion had no anti-aircraft machine guns or cannons. Since we had these with us during our recent maneuver, why did we not have them now? Destroying our supply trucks would incapacitate the tank division that depended on us. I voiced my concerns to our commanding officer who was also very distressed about our vulnerability. He told me that he was trying to get such protection as soon as possible. It took two days before three armored personal carriers – vintage Second World War vehicles retrofitted to carry two anti-aircraft guns – arrived. They were stationed on top of the hills overlooking our encampment. They indeed made a difference, not only because they opened fire on attacking Egyptian bombers, but also because their presence provided a psychological boost. We finally felt that we didn't have to rely on our personal weapons to repel the enemy.

The attacks by the Egyptian air-force did not cease. Two MiG 19 jets returned about the same time almost every day, always arriving from the same direction. They were old vintage fighter bombers, apparently used by the Egyptians mainly as bombers. A newer version of the MiG fighter jets series, MiG 21, was used by the Egyptians as fighters. I joked to my medics that the Egyptian pilots probably finished their afternoon tea and then took off to attack. In fact, I assumed that they just waited for the sun to get low so that it would be on their backs and in our eyes when they attacked. Nevertheless, the reliability of their timing enabled us to get ready every day around two o'clock in the afternoon, taking cover in the ditches and opening rifle fire when they approached. One of the medics watched the western horizon every day at the expected time in order to warn us. Despite their regularity, these attacks were still a very unnerving experience that continually left me shaken. The jets always came without any warning; because they were flying low and did not make a sound until they had already attacked, they were difficult to spot. Miraculously, except for the first one none of these attacks caused any damage.

On the fifth day of the war we were experiencing the familiar assault when a fighter jet suddenly approached from the west. It was flying quite high and I could see its silhouette. I was familiar with the silhouette of jet fighters and was convinced that this was a French made Mirage. Although this type of jet was flown by the Israeli air force it was difficult to see whether the jet had a Star of David on its wings, Israeli jets usually flew in pairs; and seeing a single jet made it unlikely that this was a friendly aircraft. As it approached, I could see that that it was painted silver, like Israeli jets. The silver color shined as the plane flew closer and closer. I was still not sure whether it was the enemy or an Israeli jet. Suddenly, it dove, discharging two bombs about three kilometers north of us, leaving an eruption of fire. We wondered if we were being mistakenly attacked by our own air force – or had an Israeli jet attacked an enemy target?

The identity of the plane remained a mystery until I learned a few hours later that we had actually been attacked by a Libyan Mirage fighter. That attack had inflicted casualties on a convoy of our tanks. Apparently the Libyans had sent two squadrons of Mirage 5 fighters to support the Egyptians. I realized that we could no longer rely on the familiar silhouette of a jet to identify its nationality. Even a familiar looking Mirage could be deadly. Fortunately, the Libyans did not return.

The daily attacks eventually ended after a final one on October the 14th. Two jets appeared as always, but this time they flew much lower than usual and did not fire or discharge any bombs. Within a fraction of a second, it became clear why. Before we had time to understand what was happening, two Israeli jets appeared, chasing and firing at the MiGs with their cannons. Some of the shells exploded a short distance away from us. Apparently, the MiGs were running for their lives this time and did not even try to attack, as they had been intercepted and chased by the faster Israeli jets. The MiGs had been attempting to evade the cannon fire by flying low. The first Israeli jet fired above the first Egyptian plane, forcing it to fly very low; within seconds, the Egyptian jet crashed into the hills and blew up in a ball of fire. We saw no evidence that anyone had ejected from the plane. The second Egyptian jet was able to avoid a direct assault, but was hit by the second Israeli Mirage jet which gave chase as the MiG made a wide turn on its attempt to return to Egypt.

We all cheered as we watched the second MiG crash in the hill and exploding in a huge fireball. *We finally got the bastards!* It was such a relief to be rescued from these repeated and unpreventable attacks that perpetuated our vulnerability. We finally watched the attackers become the attacked; the tables were finally reversed.

I doubted that the first Egyptian pilot had survived. Nevertheless, I immediately drove to the crash site, about half a kilometer down the road. In the event the pilot was still alive I wanted to help him. I was also curious to see the downed jet that had been attacking us so frequently. I hiked over sand dunes to the crash site about three hundred meters from the main road and found only a pile of burned and twisted metal. I was disappointed that there was nothing that could be done for the pilot. Again, I had mixed feelings of pride and sorrow. I was proud that our air force had returned to the sky, but was also sorry for the loss of life. I remembered the young Israeli pilots who had brought in their sick children to Kaplan Hospital. They had wives and young children. I wondered who the Egyptian pilot had left behind.

After that incident we were never again attacked. Because the war in the northern front had begun to turn in Israel's favor, the air force was finally able to divert resources to the southern front. Apparently the Egyptians did not want to challenge our pilots again and therefore did not send their jets for another assault. After the day of the attack, we routinely saw Israeli jets fly above us in the direction of the canal. To avoid the deadly Russian made SAM anti aircraft missiles the jets would zigzag as they intermittently discharged flares to mislead any missiles directed at them. We often observed anti-aircraft missiles exploding a distance away from the jets. Yet every time I saw an Israeli plane attempting to avoid an approaching missile, I became very apprehensive, hoping that it would escape. Fortunately, all the fired missiles that I observed missed their targets and our jets kept on flying. I was aware, however, that we were able to see only a limited section of the skies. The desert was large and I hoped that our jets were safe – especially in places we could not observe.

Chapter 10
Religion in War

I grew up in a secular, but traditional, Jewish family. Although both of my parents were products of typical orthodox families in Eastern Europe, they became secular once they immigrated to British Palestine in the nineteen thirties. Nevertheless, they continued to go to the synagogue on the high holidays and kept kosher. My father's five older siblings continued to observe Orthodox practices; one of his cousins was even a rabbi in a Jerusalem yeshiva. Because I was exposed to Orthodox family members, I always felt a kinship toward observant Jews. Although I never met my grandparents (they had been killed in the Holocaust), pictures showing them dressed in traditional religious clothing made me feel even closer to the Orthodox tradition. I always felt gratitude to those who kept Judaism alive during the two thousand year Diaspora.

The power of religion became evident to me in times of distress, even as a youngster. When I was sixteen years old, my four year old sister fell ill with polio and was hospitalized in Rambam Hospital in Haifa. Although my parents and I visited her daily, we were not allowed to see her because she was in medical isolation. Her condition became more serious as her paralysis progressed to her legs. Late one Friday afternoon my desperate father asked the attending pediatrician if there was anything that could be done to reverse her grave situation. The physician shrugged, noting, "The only thing that you can do is pray."

His answer disappointed me. I was already intent on becoming a physician and still believed that medicine could cure everything.

I was skeptical that praying would make any difference. Nevertheless, feeling powerless to do anything else, we followed the doctor's suggestion. My father and I went to the synagogue the next morning and recited the prayer for healing the sick. When we returned to the hospital later that day we finally heard some good news — the paralysis had stopped progressing and my sister's condition began to improve. I knew this turn of events might have happened even if we would have not prayed, but I felt in my heart that our prayers had indeed made a difference. My sister's condition continued to improve in the ensuing days and she recovered almost fully from her paralysis.

Religion played a major role throughout the war, not only because it began on Yom Kippur but also because many of our soldiers were observant Jews. Certainly the circumstances of war brought to the fore, both for the religious and non-observant among us, many of the values and inner strength that were derived from our Jewish religion and beliefs.

One of the trucks in our regiment was designated as the synagogue. It was an ordinary canopy-covered gray colored civilian truck carrying an ark containing a Torah scroll and many prayer books. The truck was parked facing Jerusalem, thus enabling the soldiers to pray as they faced the holy city. Whenever we were not on the move or under attack, a routine developed. Three times a day men would gather behind the truck for the morning, noon, and evening prayers. These were unannounced spontaneous gatherings conducted by several soldiers familiar with reciting the prayers.

The truck was parked a short distance from our van and I noticed that the number of soldiers attending the daily prayers increased over time. Most of the people in the battalion were not religiously observant; however, during the holiday of Succoth (Feast of Tabernacles) more and more soldiers were coming to the prayers throughout the seven days of the holiday. This festival commemorates the fragile dwellings, called "sukkot," in which the ancient Israelites dwelt during their fourty years of wandering in the Sinai desert. Jews around the world construct and eat in similar huts during the holiday. A Sukkah was erected in the synagogue truck and many soldiers had their meals inside, as is customary. Branches of desert brush were used as the traditional roof of the sukkah and the military rabbinate provided the battalion with the Succoth Holiday's Four Species (Etrog, Lulav. Hadassim, and Aravot). It felt surreal to observe soldiers marking the holiday despite the war around us. Yet routine religious observances and traditions gave everyone a sense of normalcy and strength. It occurred to me how meaningful it was that we were celebrating an event that our ancestors had experienced over three thousand years ago in Sinai in the same area, probably not far away from where we were standing.

I assumed that more soldiers turned to prayer and religion because of the great threat we faced. The atmosphere among the congregants was quite gloomy and reflected our dire situation. I watched soldiers as they prayed, holding their prayer books in their hands, carrying their rifles on their shoulders, and wearing their helmets instead of their yarmulkes (kippas). They faced the north–east, toward Jerusalem, and some moved their body in harmony with their chanting. I could feel from the intensity of their motions that they were trying to convey a message to God, perhaps asking for His help in these difficult times.

I was jealous of these individuals who could truly believe in the ability of God to help us. Being a non-observant Jew, like most Israelis, I was unable to draw any strength from prayers, too busy doing other things that, at the time, seemed more important. However, I could sense the effect of prayer on the religious soldiers. Their spirits were uplifted after they prayed and they projected a sense of optimism which radiated to others. Moreover, the respite from their regular activity and the ability to return to their traditions in the company of others must have invigorated them. It became clear to me that they had the ability to draw on resources I lacked, making it easier for them to live through the difficult times. They had access to a deep belief in the power of God to help in this challenging period. On the other hand, I was assessing our situation and basing my beliefs solely on what I knew was happening around us and at the war fronts. They had the capacity to stay optimistic, even when things were difficult and the news from the front was bad, while I remained somber and generally pessimistic.

Two of my medics, Zvika and Shmuel, were religiously observant. I watched them draw strength from sources not available to more secular soldiers. On one of the direst days of the war, when we had narrowly escaped a close call by enemy artillery, we spent the night at the Tassa Military Base. We were very tired and emotionally shaken from the day's experiences. As I was resting by the side of our van, Zvika and Shmuel approached, their faces glowing. I could not understand what had made them so happy. Nothing that had happened that day justified their expressions. In fact, it was something else entirely:

"We just heard that Rabbi Goren is here tonight and is going to give a sermon to the soldiers. We'd really like to hear him if you'll allow us to go."

Although I didn't want my medics to leave for very long, I felt that I could not deny them the opportunity to listen to Rabbi Goren, the Chief Rabbi of Israel and the previous Chief Rabbi of the army. He was revered as the first rabbi to reach the Western Wall (Kotel) carrying Holy Scrolls after Israeli paratroopers had liberated it during the Six Day War. They were excited and eager to hear the rabbi; I sensed that the experience would help them in ways I could not completely comprehend at that moment.

They returned about an hour later. Shmuel's face was shining with a sense of revelation and he wore a huge smile. It was an unusual sight to see anyone smiling on that day.

"The Rabbi told us that everything is going to be all right. God is behind us and we are destined to win the war."

He was assured and confident of the rabbi's promise – evidently, there was no doubt in his mind that the Israeli army would be victorious. Zvika echoed his friend's convictions. Although I was skeptical about such assurances, I did not want to spoil Zvikas' and Shmuels' beliefs. *Things are so difficult for us. How can the Rabbi promise anything?* I quietly thought to myself. Secretly I wished I could find the same level of comfort as they did, but, unfortunately, I could not. My world was grounded on realistic and concrete facts; furthermore, I strongly believed that God helped only those who helped themselves. I did not want to be like my ancestors who, living in the Diaspora, relied only on prayers for their salvation and did not actively defend themselves from evil. History taught me that this approach would only lead to disaster. I did not want to believe naively that things would turn out in our favor just by praying and neglecting the reality of the situation. The lesson I learned from Jewish history was that one must analyze the situation logically, instead of relying purely on spiritual sources.

On the Sabbath and other holidays, Zvika and Shmuel worked just as hard as the rest of us, asking for only one exemption: they wanted to avoid riding in our cars on those days unless it was part of our military movement. I tried to accommodate them whenever possible. However, when I occasionally asked them to ride during Sabbath or holidays, Zvika would always challenge me. He repeatedly asked whether driving was necessary as part of our medical work or whether it was for non medical reasons and thus could be postponed. I repeatedly explained that everything we did was related to our military mission, and since we were at war, driving superseded the sanctity of the Sabbath. I never won these arguments; Zvika always made his own decisions, according to his own standards, when to get on a car on a Sabbath or a holiday. Shmuel, on the other hand, did not protest the need to drive on the Sabbath.

As an officer, I felt powerless when my orders were not followed. This created tension between Zvika and me, and I resented his refusal to obey my orders. However, since many of my relatives were also observant Jews, I nevertheless respected his convictions and let him make his own choices. Fortunately, I was able to use other medics on these occasions.

As difficult as Zvika could be on these occasions, an unexpected incident illuminated an aspect of him and the strength of his beliefs that I never knew existed.

On the 11th of October we evacuated a soldier who had sustained a fracture of his hand to the Baluza military base. Two medics, Zvika and Ehud, joined our driver, Avi, and me on this twelve kilometer ride. Just after we brought the soldier to the medical facility and were turning around to return to our battalion, the general alarm siren sounded. Within a few seconds the base loudspeakers announced, "Take cover immediately. A missile attack is imminent." This came as a complete surprise. I had initially felt safe inside the large military base, but suddenly realized that we were even more vulnerable to an enemy who was targeting the base with missiles.

We knew that the Egyptians and Syrians were equipped with Frog missiles which had a range of seventy kilometers. These missiles had already reached several Israeli rear bases and inflicted numerous casualties. We were able to observe them flying over our heads on several occasions at night because their illuminating jet engine burners identified their positions. They looked like slow moving stars in the sky. On one occasion our battalion's anti-aircraft battery hit a missile and it fell, exploding several miles away from us like a meteor.

Knowing how devastating a missile strike could be, I took no chances and ordered our driver to stop the van near the closest underground shelter. Everyone around us stopped what they were doing and rushed to take shelter. There was no way of knowing when and where the missile would hit. We quickly jumped out of the van and ran into the bunker. The only thing I took was my Uzi from which I was never separated. It had been ingrained in me throughout my military service that "One never leaves a soldier or gun behind." At that moment I thought that I did not need to take anything else.

Once we entered the darkened bunker I searched for my driver and medics. The place was full of people but as soon as my eyes adjusted to the darkness I realized that everyone was accounted for except Zvika.

As we anxiously waited for the missile to hit, I kept expecting Zvika to show up. Minutes that felt like hours passed and he was still missing. I became increasingly more worried and finally walked out of the shelter to look for him. The whole base was deserted, as everyone had taken cover when the siren sounded. Then, in the middle of the eerily silent base, I spotted Zvika standing behind the rear doors of the van, calmly unloading the medical backpacks that we always carried. He seemed completely oblivious to the danger he was facing.

I was very upset that he had ignored the order to get inside the bunker and shouted, "What are you doing?! Come into the shelter immediately! Don't you know that a missile may hit the base any second?"

Instead of heeding my order, Zvika ignored me. He slowly and meticulously placed one medical backpack on his shoulders, grabbed the other two in his hands, and brought them to the bunker, walking at a maddeningly leisurely pace. His slow steps infuriated me, considering the grave danger we were facing.

"What are you doing? Don't you realize that a missile attack is imminent?? You need to get into the bunker as soon as possible!" I shouted at him angrily.

"I took our medical backpacks with us," he answered. "They were in the van underneath other equipment and I need to move other stuff to get to them. In case the base is hit and the van damaged, we won't have any medical supplies. How can we be of any help if we don't have our medical backpacks?"

I was stunned but immediately understood why he had ignored my orders to get into the bunker. I realized that he had a higher moral standard than I did. While I had been thinking only about protecting my own life, he was able to think beyond his own safety and risk his life, remembering that his duty as a medic was to care for others. My attitude toward Zvika changed entirely from that moment. His refusal to travel on Sabbath was a miniscule nuisance compared to his inner strength and compassion for others.

"Weren't you afraid that you were risking your life" I asked.

To which he answered, "It is in the hands of God if I live or die. I have just to do the right thing."

At that moment I realized that a strong belief in an all-knowing God helped Zvika overcome whatever fear he might have felt. Yet I was still of the opinion such an approach could keep one from being able to judge each situation on its merits. I firmly believed that our survival depended on making logical decisions to enhance our chance to stay alive. I was taught in my medical officers' course that, whenever possible, I should not put my medical unit at unnecessary risks. If anyone under my command would be injured or killed, the ability to care for our troops would suffer. This message was on my mind throughout the campaign and influenced many of my decisions.

I noticed on several occasions that both Zvika and Shmuel shared the belief that their fate rested in God's hands. They expressed this conviction when we discussed our general situation and also exhibited it in their actions. They were often willing to take risks that I considered unwarranted. I had to stop them on several occasions from risking both their own and the lives of others. On one occasion we had to choose which road to take to return to our battalion. The shorter way was deserted and thus prone to an Egyptian commando attack. I elected to take the longer road, which took about half an hour more of travel time but was well traveled by other vehicles. Shmuel tried to persuade me to take the shorter, less traveled road so that we could return to our battalion sooner in case there were sick or injured who needed us.

Another time we encountered enemy artillery bombarding the road ahead of us. I elected to stop and wait for the shelling to end before resuming the drive, although both Zvika and Shmuel argued for proceeding ahead and taking our chances in the face of obvious danger.

Religion was a powerful force that definitely influenced some of my medics. Fortunately, we were able to find the right balance between the secular and the spiritual as the war ensued.

Chapter 11
Fear

On the third day of the war, I confronted a new enemy: fear and anxiety among the troops. I was unprepared to face an issue that I had never dealt with before.

We were stationed on the road side waiting for orders to resume our drive forward when a jeep, heralded by the sound of squeaking brakes and driven by the Sergeant Major, stopped by our van.

"Doc, you have to come with me right away!"

"What's the problem?"

"It's the Deputy Commanding Officer's driver. He and the Deputy Commander returned from the front where they were caught by enemy bombardment. After letting the Deputy get off the jeep, the driver told him that he was going to leave the battalion and drive back to his home in Tel Aviv. He than drove away by himself, finally being intercepted by our rear guard at the end of our convoy. He's acting very strangely and says that he's leaving and returning home."

I was surprised that I was asked to deal with the issue. *After all,* I thought, *This is an administrative and conduct problem, not a medical one.* On the other hand, I could not exclude a psychological reason behind such an action. As a medical officer, I was required to take care of the soldiers' mental, as well as their physical health.

I responded without any delay, taking off immediately in our van along with one of my medics. When we arrived at the jeep, near a road intersection a few kilometers from Baluza, I found the driver calmly sitting in the driver's seat, smoking a cigarette, with the engine running. He was a man in his thirties whose uniform was immaculate and black hair was nicely combed.

"What is going on? Why do you want to leave?" I asked.

"I've had enough of this war. I can't take it anymore," he calmly replied. "I'm leaving and this is it."

I pressed him: "What is it that you can't take any more?" He did not respond, but kept shifting the gears back and forth, still smoking his cigarette and gunning the engine as if about to drive away any second.

This was the first time I had encountered a soldier intent on deserting and even openly admitting it. My first thought was to have him arrested for desertion, but no one was there to detain him. I assumed that he was afraid and perhaps traumatized by his recent experiences but did not know how to express his anxiety. I could sympathize with his sensation of fear, as I had been afraid from the moment we arrived at the front but, like everyone else, kept my emotions to myself. We lived in a society where admission of fear was a taboo, incompatible with masculinity. At that stage of the war, I was uncomfortable, disappointed, and even ashamed of myself for feeling that way and did not yet know how to properly approach this topic with someone else.

I realized that I could not argue with the driver or order him to abandon his plan to leave. Rather, I decided to incapacitate him by injecting him with a sedative. I turned to my medic and asked him to give me a syringe with valium. But when I turned back toward the driver, his jeep disappeared in a cloud of dust. Everyone around me was apparently stunned by this sudden turn of events. No one attempted to chase the fleeing man, and within moments, he and his jeep were tiny dots on the horizon. We did not see him again throughout the war and I became too preoccupied with other issues to even inquire about his whereabouts. The master sergeant, who witnessed the entire episode, was unprepared to deal with the situation.

We exchanged a few words, trying to understand what had happened. No one had seen this coming, according to the master sergeant. The driver had served in our battalion for a couple of years, was extremely dependable, and had never exhibited erratic behavior. Not knowing what else to do, I got back into the van and returned to our place in the convoy.

As we drove away, I felt both frustrated and embarrassed because of my inability to stop the driver. I assumed that he would eventually be apprehended by the military police and would be court-martialed for desertion. Yet I could not be sure this would be the outcome because of the confusion and the mounting problems that we were all encountering. Certainly the surrounding chaos of the war might prevent the execution of proper military procedures in apprehending a single deserter. In retrospect, I could have handled the situation differently by recognizing the soldier's condition as psychological in nature. However, his demeanor was so composed and he was so logical and determined that I did not suspect any mental problem. Even in the midst of battle, it is very difficult to prevent someone who is determined to leave.

The constant danger was especially evident in the behavior of the soldiers who drove or escorted fuel tankers and ammunition trucks to the front. Several of the drivers requested tranquilizers to quell their anxiety. Some described in detail what they were doing to refuel or provide ammunition to the fighting tanks.

I remember the first time that a fuel tanker driver talked to me about his experiences and asked for help. This man, in his thirties, came by late in the afternoon. We sat facing each other on the sand by the side of the van. He was tall and muscular with a receding hair line. His hair was dusted with sand and his uniform and his face were blackened with oil. He looked exhausted but was serious and somber. He told me in an almost whispery voice what he had been doing in the past few days.

"I've been driving my fuel tanker to the front line several times every day, spending hours refueling the tanks. The crews engaged in heavy fighting would drive over to me in turn. Since they didn't want to leave the line of fire unprotected, they came one at a time. I would wait for them to retreat and, once they got close to me, I would jump out of my seat, tow the fueling pipe, insert it into the gas tank, and begin refueling. Oftentimes there were artillery explosions or heavy machine gun fire around me. However, despite what was going on around me, I had to keep on with the refueling process, one tank after another."

I was completely unprepared to hear his story. I had never realized the danger faced by the drivers of our battalion. As he continued to talk and gesture with his hands, I observed the oil and blackened grease on his palms. They bore silent testimony to the kind of work he was engaged in.

"Is there anything that you can do to avoid being hit by enemy fire?" I asked what seemed to me to be a stupid question.

"Most of the time I can't do anything about it – I just hope to be lucky. Sometimes I park my truck behind a hill, if there is one, so that the enemy won't spot me, but I often get confused by the dust and noise around me and I can't even tell where the enemy is actually firing from."

"What can I do to help you?" I asked, trying to be practical.

He replied in a quite and almost apologetic voice: "I know that what I'm doing is dangerous, but I have to do it. The tank crews depend on me and are always very happy to see me. Because I bring them the fuel that allows them to keep fighting, they look at me as their savior. I just want you to give me a few pills of Valium so I can take one when things get rough. I'm always terrified in the midst of the firefight and I'm constantly afraid that my truck will be hit and explode. Maybe valium will help me ignore my fear."

His story shook me. Over and over again he was a hero. His sincere admission of fear was so understandable and human, and his request for a pill to assist him in his heroism seemed logical to me. How could I deny him?

Yet I was afraid that by giving him a tranquilizer I might endanger his life. His survival depended on his ability to navigate a gasoline-loaded truck on the road and on the battlefield. His judgment might be impaired if he couldn't function at full capacity under the influence of a drug. I tried to convey these risks to him.

"I can give you Valium pills but these may make you tired and impair your thinking. Being afraid may keep you alive if your fear forces you to avoid being harmed. Taking the pill is risky in many ways. Are you sure you want it?"

He thought for a minute and replied:

"I understand these risks and promise to take a pill only when I feel that I really need it."

I gave him a couple of pills and asked him to return and see me if he needed more or had any other problems. He did not return to see me again.

His story was typical of those I heard from other drivers in the ensuing days. They recounted how they would drive their fuel or ammunition-loaded trucks to the rear of the battle line and wait for the tanks to retreat, their turrets still facing the enemy until they reached the tankers or ammunition trucks. The drivers would refuel the tanks or load them with ammunition as the battle raged on only a short distance away. After refueling or reloading, the tanks would drive forward and rejoin the fighting. These refueling and ammunition replenishment tasks were very dangerous and the drivers who performed them were indeed very brave. By the end of the war, several had been injured or killed. I did not take care of those soldiers who were evacuated directly to the field hospital by the physicians of the tank battalions.

On occasions when the refueling and ammunition trucks could not navigate the treacherous sand dunes they waited for the tanks to come to them on the main roads. The trucks sometimes had to wait for hours at the margin of the battlefield to allow for all the tanks to refuel and reloaded their ammunition. On October 10, which happened to be a very difficult day of fighting, one of the drivers told me how our supply vehicles had driven to Spontani Road, a distance of about two kilometers from the battle zone. Because of the fierce fighting and difficult terrain, they could not reach the tanks and waited until the brigade's commanders sent armored troop carriers backward to the main road. Upon their arrival, they were loaded with fuel and ammunition and sent back to the tanks.

On another occasion, at two o'clock on the afternoon of October 11, our refueling and ammunition trucks were attacked by Egyptian airplanes on Ma'adim Road, about fifteen kilometers from the front. Trying to avoid being stuck in the sandy dunes, all the supply vehicles and tanks remained on the main road. Tragically, such an obvious location made them an easy target from the air and many tank crews and tanker drivers were killed or injured in the bombing runs. After that battle, the wounded were evacuated directly to the field hospital in the Refidim Base, which meant that I did not treat them. It was only that evening that I heard about the harrowing events of that day from the surviving drivers.

Navigating their volatile cargo in the battlefield took guts, yet none of the drivers (except for the one instance described earlier) asked to be relieved of his duties or discharged. While I could not refuse the request of the handful of soldiers who requested tranquilizers, I always warned them that taking this medication might impair their judgment; in the end, several decided not to take the drugs. I ended up carrying Valium pills in my shirt pocket so that I could dispense them when I made my morning drives.

Despite the ongoing risks, only a handful of drivers came to me to discuss their fears. Many more, I'm sure, felt extreme angst while working under fire and handling explosives and gasoline. Yet they must have dealt with their personal fears on their own, perhaps by speaking with their comrades or by just suppressing their anxiety. It could also be that they were unable to reach me because our battalion was spread over a great distance on several roads.

Another reason that might have accounted for the small number of drivers who sought help for their fears was the prevailing culture in Israeli society, where admitting fear was virtually a taboo. A man was expected to be strong and fearless. Admitting fear was regarded as cowardly and not a realistic or normal response to danger.

I was tempted at times to take a tranquilizer myself but decided against it. I was afraid that my judgment would be impaired if I did so. I felt strongly that I needed to maintain all my senses, not only to ensure the survival of my medical unit, but also to be able to make correct medical decisions.

Initially, I had great difficulty dealing with soldiers who asked for help in handling their anxieties and fear. I had no training in the diagnosis and treatment of the psychological impact of war. Even though I had completed the medical officer training five years earlier, my instructors never mentioned the syndrome of Post Traumatic Stress Disorder (PTSD). I think the reason for this lack of training is that Israel's previous two wars were short and victorious. No one was prepared for a longer war in which we did not have the initiative. No one was prepared for dealing with soldiers who were faced with the possibility of losing.

I was very surprised and disappointed in myself when I first sensed my own fear, feeling as though I had failed myself. Since no one talked about it, I assumed that I was different from the rest of my comrades who, I believed, knew no fear.

No one else is afraid. There must be something wrong with me for feeling fear, I thought.

I had always been confident in my ability to deal with physical danger. Because of my past training in sharpshooting, fencing and boxing I was confident in my ability to handle a person-to-person confrontations with an enemy. I was trained to seek out the enemy and to eliminate the source of danger rather than to be passive or run away. I had actually faced such a confrontation during the Six Day War when I evacuated wounded paratroopers from the Old City of Jerusalem to Hadassah Medical Center. I was working in the emergency room of Hadassah Medical Center in Jerusalem where many wounded soldiers and civilians were sent for treatment. I would on occasion go out with the ambulances to evacuate the wounded to the hospital. On one occasion, a Jordanian sniper opened fire on our loading area from a nearby building. As the fire rained down, I borrowed an Uzi submachine gun from one of the wounded soldiers. Together with another soldier, we entered the building where we suspected the sniper was hiding. With our weapons drawn, we opened every door. We expected to confront and shoot at the sniper on every floor. Eventually, the firing stopped, although we never found the sniper. While I sensed some apprehension during that incident, the prospect of remaining passive and just taking cover was not an option. Seeking and removing the threat were, in my mind, the right things to do.

What I was not prepared for was the exposure to danger from an unseen enemy. I felt that way even in the Six Day War when Hadassah hospital was shelled from the Jordanian West Bank. Yet I was able to handle some precarious situations better than others. Although frightened when we were attacked from the air, I could cope reasonably well because I could see the jets come and go, take cover when necessary, and even fire my weapon. On the other hand, being attacked by distant artillery or missiles was difficult to get used to. I had no control over the source of the danger and could not eliminate it. Facing danger caused by circumstances I had no control of was far more difficult than dealing with those I could control.

I realized the limitations of training and courage in modern warfare, as I could not rely on my own abilities to save my life. In fact, most people are injured or die because they happen to be at the wrong place at the wrong time.

Fortunately our exposure to danger increased gradually. Over time I adjusted to a higher threat level. As it happened, there were a few days between each of the threat escalations. Initially, we were at risk because of our proximity to the fighting. As the days progressed, we worried about commando attacks, then aerial attacks, and, finally, our perilous crossing over the Suez Canal into Egypt.

One of my earliest challenges was dealing with the anxiety and stress disorder experienced by Avner, one of my medics. On the fourth day of the war, he suddenly started to exhibit bizarre behavior. He would stay up all night and remain on watch, even when his turn was over. He was lying on his stomach and aiming his rifle in the direction of the surrounding hills, while whispering that he could see Egyptian commandos preparing an assault on us. Our assurances that there was no invisible commando unit did not help. Consistently anxious, he was convinced that there was an unseen danger and he became increasingly disconnected from the reality around him.

I had known Avner for over three years as a quiet person and a dependable medic. About two years earlier he had called me before our annual training and asked to meet in person. When he arrived at Kaplan Hospital, where I was working, he had a very unusual request. He told me that he had just gotten into a new business venture: distributing music albums. Attending our upcoming three week training session, he explained, would have devastating consequences on his business. He had just gotten married and had invested all his savings into the venture. His official request to the military to be excused from the battalion's training exercise had been denied. He wondered if I could find a way to help him and suggested that I contact or write a letter to the battalion's recruiting office telling them that I could manage without him.

I understood his predicament and wanted to help him. I was intensely loyal to my medics and treated them as if they were part of my family. I had invited them to our apartment for an evening together after each of our battalion's maneuvers. Avner's request, though, was unique. I knew how hard he had worked throughout his life and did not want to see him fail. Although he was an integral part of our team, I knew that I could get along with one less medic, especially since we would only be engaged in a training exercise. Since he owned his own business and was not employed by others, he was clearly at a risk of suffering irreparable damage if he had to close for three weeks. The other medics were not subject to such a situation because they were either students or were employees of large companies which could get along without them. I also knew that if I had to go through official channels to try to relieve Avner, his request would undoubtedly be denied again.

I decided to assume the responsibility for excusing Avner myself and told him to show up on the designated day. I wanted him to travel with us to our training site, but I promised that I would excuse him if I judged that our work burden and assignments could be managed without him. He would then be able to leave us until the conclusion of the exercise, at which time he would have to come back to the training site and return with us to the base to be officially discharged with the rest of us.

While I knew I was taking a risk, I thought that not allowing him the time off could be devastating for him. I did not dwell on the fact that I may have been breaking the rules, but I felt that loyalty to my medics was of paramount importance. If I expected them to risk their lives during war time, I had to do my best to help them in their time of need. As his immediate supervisor, I understood his unique situation; the anonymous military establishment could not be so flexible.

Luckily, our plan worked. Avner was able to return home during the exercise and no one except me and my medics knew about the arrangement. We were a very close knit group which did what needed to be done to help each other. The other medics had to work harder to pick up Avner's slack. He called me every few days to check whether he needed to return earlier and I had his phone number in case I needed to contact him. When he came back to join us prior to our discharge, he told us how essential it had been for him to be able to continue his work during the past two weeks. He brought each of us an album of Israeli songs as a token of his gratitude. We were all so happy when, a year later on our divisional maneuvers, Avner proudly told us that his business had flourished. He thanked us again for covering for him at a critical moment in his life.

Because of what had previously happened with Avner, I did not want him to fail as a medic. I thought that I could help him get over his anxiety so that he would not have to live with a feeling of failure. I listened to his worries with an open mind and when he told me his irrational assessments of the dangers we faced, I didn't ridicule him. I tried to tell him that things were not as bad as he thought. I resisted my budding sense that the best thing for Avner would be to evacuate him. I did not want to loss one of my four medics and hoped that he would adapt to the situation. I felt that letting him leave would be a personal failure for me.

To compensate for his instability, I kept him next to me at all times. I hoped to thus be able to immediately address his worries and make him feel better. Unfortunately, he seemed to deteriorate further over time. His sleepless nights made him exhausted, his irrational behavior increased, and he often claimed that he could see Egyptians coming to attack us.

The final straw occurred when I took him with me on my daily sick call tour throughout our battalion. I did not want to leave him behind with the other medics. Because of his fragility I did not want to rely on him as my sole assistant, and also took Shmuel with us. We drove for several kilometers along a winding road through the hilly desert terrain, encountering very little traffic coming the other way. I felt a sense of isolation and tension in the air. There were reports of Egyptian commando attacks a day earlier not far away. I knew that when we ventured onto the side roads we were susceptible to ambushes by Egyptian commandos.

Watching Avner's face as we drove, I soon realized that I made a mistake taking him with me on this potentially risky drive. He was silent and perspiring as he clutched his rifle with great intensity. After about thirty minutes —which felt more like an hour — we finally reached the ammunition company. It was a relief to see the long convoy of trucks parked one after the other on the side of the road. That lifeline of the fighting forces was highly vulnerable and I was happy to see two armored troop carriers bearing anti-aircraft guns stationed on top of the hill overlooking the road. They must have arrived the day before to protect the ammunition company from repeated attacks by the Egyptian air force.

We are finally not alone. What a relief, I thought.

We parked our van in the center of the long line of trucks where we saw a group of soldiers waiting for us.

Stern, the company commander, was there to welcome us. I was always happy to see him, as it rekindled fond memories of early childhood. We used to travel together with our fathers when their soccer team, HaPoel Haifa, played in the Jewish Palestinian Soccer league. How ironic, I thought, *We used to travel together in the soccer team's truck, since bus travel was a luxury the soccer club could not afford. Here we are again, twenty-seven years later, in the middle of the desert meeting by the side of a convoy of trucks.*

"I'm happy to see that you finally received anti-aircraft batteries," I told Stern. In the rush to the front the need to provide such protection was overlooked and I knew that he had been requesting it for several days.

"Yes, what a relief. I had to keep complaining to finally get these two batteries. There are not enough of them around. We have several sick soldiers today. Nothing major," Stern said.

"I'm organizing the supply convoy to the front and can't stay with you now," he apologized. "I'll try to see you before you leave."

The sick soldiers were already waiting for us and I immediately began to assess their medical problems. Avner, who was supposed to be helping me, stood away from us looking at the horizon, seemingly distracted by something. I did not continue to watch him and turned away to talk to my patient.

A few minutes later I looked again toward Avner and to my astonishment saw that he had collapsed. He was lying on the side of the road in the fetal position, shivering and mumbling incoherently. He did not respond to my attempts to communicate with him and kept muttering fragmented sentences.

The episode was very disturbing and upsetting. I was shaken to see Avner in such a state of agitation. His collapse in front of soldiers of the ammunition company exposed them to a difficult sight. Seeing a medic collapse in front of those he came to help is especially hard to digest.

Shmuel and I immediately injected Avner with sedatives and placed him on a stretcher. He calmed down within a minute and we put the stretcher in the van and took off immediately to evacuate him to the closest field hospital. As we dropped him off at the field hospital in Baluza, I realized I should have recognized the severity of Avner's condition earlier. I felt bad that by waiting a few days I contributed to his mental collapse and misjudged my ability to effectively help him by keeping him close to me.

I learned only later that his reaction was a classic case of PTSD, the best treatment for which is temporary removal from the stressful environment. Most people need only a few days of reprieve, accompanied by counseling. I later understood that my failure to help Avner was also due to my inability at that time to speak openly to him about the validity of his fears and to reassure him that it was normal to be afraid. By not validating his anxieties, I left him as the only one among us who openly expressed his fears. Even though I also felt afraid at times, I kept my thoughts to myself.

My initial reaction to the soldiers who sought help for their fears was to deny them the right to admit their worries. Most bore a look of shame and spoke quietly as they confided their anxiety. Nearly all felt that something was wrong with them and they kept their voices low so that no one would hear their confessions. I used the model of John Wayne's response to the Marines in the movie "Green Beret" and told them to be tough and strong like Wayne's character, Colonel Mike Kirby, and get back to their duties.

Inside, I felt that what I was doing was inappropriate and that I was not addressing the problem at hand. Denying them the right to admit the existence of fear rendered their right to be afraid illegitimate. This attitude confirmed the soldiers' inner conviction that something in them was wrong. I had failed to help these individuals and was haunted by the shameful and anxious looks in their eyes when they left. Their visits to me perhaps brought them temporary relief, yet did not provide them with any tools to cope with their fears.

Despite my dawning comprehension that what I was doing was not working, I did not know what else to do. I was still operating under the dogma that fear was an unnatural feeling a soldier is not supposed to have. I was also disappointed in, and ashamed of, myself for having similar feelings. I was convinced that my reaction to the situation was abnormal and should be concealed.

After a few days of increasing frustration with my inability to help the soldiers deal with their anxieties, it suddenly dawned on me that I should not deny the fact that I shared the same feelings. This insight came to me as I was listening to a soldier confess his fears and anxieties. As I listened, seeing the shame and guilt in his face, I realized that he was actually describing my own feelings. I could not pretend anymore and decided to break the code of silence and denial that I had imposed on myself. *Yes, I am also afraid,* I admitted to myself.

This was a new revelation that I decided to share with the soldier.

"I'm as frightened as you are. How could I not be?" I said. "Shells are falling on us, airplanes are strafing us, commando soldiers are looking for us, and missiles are flying in our direction. It's completely natural to be afraid."

I immediately saw the relief spread out on the soldier's face. He was saying without words, *If the doctor who is also an officer is telling me that it's OK to be afraid then there's nothing wrong with me.*

I finally broke the taboo against admitting my own fear and sanctioning the idea that fear is normal in dangerous situations. This time I realized that I was actually helping my patient and that he clearly felt much better after our discussion. His fear was not gone, but it was legitimized and accepted as a normal and even necessary feeling, not something that has to be hidden and ashamed of.

It occurred to me that fear could be my friend – as long as I was cautious and responsible. It also seemed to me that our adversaries were probably just as afraid as we were. This conflict is between frightened groups of people, on both sides of the front, who were all wearing military uniforms. The war would be won by the side which could still perform despite its natural fear. Fear, I remembered from reading my psychiatry textbook, could cause three reactions: it could send you running away; it could freeze you in your tracks; or it could make you charge forward to eliminate its source.

From that moment onward, I began to alter my approach when I addressed fear related issues with my patients. I shared with them the fact that I was just as afraid as they were. "It's okay to be afraid," I told them. I almost always observed in their faces the same relief as I had seen in the face of the first soldier to whom I admitted my own fear. I told them that they were not less manly by admitting their fear. Then I explained their choices in coping with their fear, leaving it to them to decide how to do so. Most of the time a short talk was enough to relieve their burden, and almost all felt able to go back to their duties. A few needed some anti-anxiety medication, and a handful had to be evacuated.

I found out that not only was I able to help others to legitimate their fears, but I was able to help myself each time I counseled a soldier. Hearing soldiers admit their fears actually made me feel better about myself because I realized that I was not alone in my anxiety. I only discovered this method of coping with a soldier's fear the hard way, out of necessity, and wished that I had done so earlier.

Chapter 12
Moving toward the Suez Canal

A stalemate had developed on our front between October 11 and 13 and a waiting mode ensued. Even though we were about fifteen kilometers east of the front, I could sense that nothing major was happening. The sounds of explosions to the west quieted down, there were fewer fuel and ammunition trucks sent to the front, and there was less traffic going westward. We had even developed a routine in our daily activity.

The news from both the northern and southern fronts became more favorable. Returning drivers reported that the Israeli military had apparently found a partial answer to the deadly hand-held anti-tank missiles that had decimated our tanks. Rather than sending unescorted tanks, it had been decided to send armored infantry soldiers on armoured personnel carriers to accompany the tanks and to infiltrate and eliminate Egyptian anti-tank batteries before Israeli tanks could be within the range of Egyptian missiles. These fast moving and agile forces were deemed to be better able to cope with the anti-tank missile threat than the tanks acting alone.

The Israeli radio was also broadcasting better news. The tide in the Golan Heights was shifting in our favor and we learned that Israeli forces had recaptured the lost territories and were pushing towards Damascus. Hearing this news boosted our morale. Perhaps we were going to reverse the onslaught and win this war as we had done in times past. Even though there was no official information to support my optimism, my gut feeling was that it was only a matter of time before we would be on the offensive and pushing the Egyptians backwards.

Because of the proximity of the Golan Heights to the center of Israel and the civilian population, I knew that stopping the advance of the Syrians was more vital for the survival of the country than winning in Sinai. This was not the case in the south where the desert served as a protective buffer for the center of the country. Only after victory in the north would the army divert its resources to fighting the Egyptians. This had also been the strategy during the Six Day War when the Golan Heights were captured only after the Egyptians and Jordanians had been defeated. A small country like Israel was limited in its ability to fight effectively on two fronts. Even though there was no official explanation, I assumed that the tremendous losses in manpower and equipment made it even more difficult to mount an effective counter-offensive on both fronts.

The relative calm disappeared on October 14. Sounds of fighting returned and urgent calls for supplies came in to our battalion. Once more, convoys of trucks began flowing westward. When I asked our deputy commanding officer what was going on, he said that the Egyptians had resumed their offensive and were attempting to advance eastward, away from their positions east of the Suez Canal. The rumor was that the Egyptians were bowing to the pressure of the Syrians to relieve some of the pressure on them.

A truck driver who had returned from the front and needed care for a burn injury to his leg was my source of information on the events of that day. His uniform, hands, and face were blackened with tar and dirt and his trousers were partially burned. He explained that he was caught in a fire while helping to evacuate an Israeli tank crew member whose tank had been hit by a handheld anti-tank missile. The Egyptians had attacked throughout the entire front. After heavy fighting, they were repelled, having suffered heavy casualties and losing more than two hundred tanks on a single day.

As I learned during my daily trips to our battalion's companies, supplies and equipment among our forces were becoming scarce. Stern, the ammunition company commander, constantly shared with me his frustration that his company was not being adequately resupplied because the military's stocks of ammunition had been exhausted. He contended that this occurred because none of the country's leaders believed that Israel would have to fight a protracted war in the near future. Apparently there were general shortages in ammunition and other supplies, as well as in aircraft and tanks. I also heard from other officers that many Israeli jets were lost to anti-aircraft missiles during the first days of the war when they attempted to stop the Egyptians from crossing the Suez Canal and the Syrians from capturing the Golan Heights.

It was a relief to hear on the radio a week into the war that the United States had begun providing military supplies and sending us aircraft and tanks to replenish those lost in battle. A few days later I began seeing our supply convoys delivering boxes of American made ammunition to replenish our dwindling resources. Unlike the Israeli-made ammunition with the Hebrew word "Ammunition" stenciled on the side, these new boxes were decorated with the American Stars and Stripes reminiscent of old war movies

For the first time we began to see camouflage-colored Israeli Phantom jet fighters with the familiar Star of David appear in the sky. Initially, I was taken aback by their unfamiliar color – Israeli jets were always painted silver. I was told by a staff officer that these jets had just been shipped from the United States and were so new that they still had their old U.S. Air Force colors. In the rush to put them into service, their only Israel identification was a six-point Star of David that had been painted over the five-pointed American star.

I was extremely grateful to the United States for standing by us during these trying times. The proverb "A friend indeed is a friend in need" was never more true. While I knew that President Nixon was currently not popular at home because of the evolving Watergate scandal, receiving the ammunition boxes with the American star and seeing the camouflage - colored Phantom jets flying overhead made me feel very thankful. He really came to our rescue at a critical time for Israel's survival.

The news about the improvement on the northern front and the successful day of fighting on October 14th made me more optimistic that we would eventually win the war. There were also signs that things were improving on our front. More Israeli jets were visible in the sky and the attacks by the Egyptian air force had ceased. The most significant sign that we would soon be on the offensive was the appearance of strange trucks in our midst, huge semi-trailers with large wheels and folding bridges mounted above the driver's cab. I had seen them during our previous exercises when they were used to build a pontoon bridge over a large pond of water representing the Suez Canal. It was clear that these trucks were each carrying parts of a pontoon bridge. Over a period of five days, starting from the sixth day of the war, we saw several of them drive by our battalion toward the canal or parked along the side of the roads at different locations. This could mean only one thing: a crossing of the Suez Canal into Egypt was imminent. Yet, no one with whom we spoke had any idea where or when it would happen.

Seeing these folding bridges uplifted everyone's spirit. They signified that we would soon be taking the initiative rather than being on the defense. I had always believed that the best defense is an effective offense and was happy that we had trained how to cross a water barrier only ten months earlier. At the time, the exercise seemed unnecessary; the idea that we would have to cross the Suez Canal was very remote. Finally, I understood the significance of that exercise.

It was the middle of the Jewish lunar month of Tishrey; the moon shone full and bright every night. It cast a glow over our battalion, which consisted of columns of trucks, dusty from repeated trips to the front lines, parked by the sides of the road. As I watched the moon sink into the horizon, I thought that it served a useful function in the war. Our attack would probably not begin until the end of the month, when the moon would appear later at night and shrink in size. A darker night would provide better conditions for a surprise attack and crossing of the canal. *It was strange,* I thought, *that our success in the war relies on the biblical way of life influenced by the stars and moon.*

My prediction came true on October 17 when we heard on the radio that Israeli forces had crossed the Suez Canal. The news was promising. General Ariel Sharon's division had been successful in crossing the canal the night before, taking advantage of the weakened Egyptian defenses between the Second and Third Egyptian Armies. We had no idea how difficult the crossing had been, although we heard about bitter fighting and numerous casualties at a place dubbed "The Chinese Farm" close to the canal.

Most of our information came via rumors and hearsay. At that time I understood again the meaning of "The Fog of War." Although we were in the midst of an all out war, we knew only what was happening as far as our eyes could see. Not knowing what was happening on the front added to everyone's anxiety and the resultant uncertainty contributed to the worry that the war was not progressing well. I constantly asked other soldiers and officers in the battalion about news from the front and sometimes even waved down passing cars to find out what was happening. I felt very frustrated not knowing the general picture. How could I make decisions about my patients and counsel others if I was uninformed? Again, I wished that my medical team had received a wireless radio.

A few hours after hearing the news about the successful canal crossing, we were told to be ready to move. Our division was to follow General Sharon's and cross into Egypt on the bridge that had been erected on the canal at the western end of the Tzir Akavish ("Scorpion Road"), north of the Bitter Lake. Apprehensive but relieved that we were finally going on the offensive, I was instructed to remain at the end of our almost three hundred vehicle convoy to take care of any medical problems. However, not having any communication equipment on board the van, I had to rely again on verbal directions sent via messengers who would drive back and forth through the convoy and deliver orders from the commanding officer.

Our driver, Avi, was reassigned to a different vehicle and we got a new driver. I was not too upset to lose Avi. He never fit in well with the rest of our team, and I sensed that he resented his chores. Our new driver, David, was in his late forties and older than the rest of us. He was a father figure, reliable and friendly. We didn't have much time to become acquainted with him before we had to start moving. Soon we realized that David's main concern was the safety and whereabouts of his nineteen year old son, a paratrooper assigned to a brigade on our front. Because Israel's precarious situation required that men remain in the reserves until their early fifties, having a father and son fighting in the same war was a common occurrence. It was, however, the first time that I had personally experienced this situation, and being a father myself, I understood David's worries, secretly happy that my son was too young to be with me in this war. I quietly hoped that there would not be a need for my son and me to serve together in the future.

We drove through Kartisan Road, and the lateral road from south of Baluza area in the northern part of the Sinai Peninsula to the central part where we passed the Tassa military base. Although the distance was only about fifty kilometers, it took us over seven hours to reach Tassa because of congestion along the road. Despite clouds of dust, I could see the large communication antennas rising above the base and observed the commotion within. I had seen Tassa during our training exercises but had never been inside. We were directed by our battalion's messenger jeep to a narrow two way road, Tzir Akavish, headed toward the Suez Canal. Apparently this was the only road leading to the canal that had been captured by Israeli forces.

Within minutes of driving on Tzir Akavish it became clear that this was a bottleneck through which every vehicle traveling toward Egypt had to pass. The thirty kilometer long asphalt road, weather beaten and severely damaged by the tracks of passing tanks, was only about seven meters wide, had no shoulders, and wound westward through sandy yellow hills. Traffic moved very slowly. The road was congested with bumper to bumper traffic as long convoys lumbered toward the front. From time to time we had to move to the side when tank transporters or huge gasoline trucks needed to pass.

A continuous flow of Patton and Centurion tanks and Zelda (M113) armored personal carriers streamed along both sides of the road creating large clouds of sand. Despite the heat, we had to roll up our windows whenever these vehicles passed. Their tracks enabled them to avoid the narrow road and travel on the sandy terrain. Occasionally we observed the familiar site of tanks with broken chains, their crews laboring to repair them, while other tanks waited to be repaired or towed away. I wondered what happens to a tank crew that had to remain behind because of a mechanical problem and how they could be reunited with their company. I was also curious about how the crews felt about being left behind. Given their vulnerability to anti-tank missile fire, perhaps these men were, in fact, glad to be late, or even avoid, getting to the front.

Most of the traffic heading away from the canal consisted of broken-down tanks towed by other tanks or tank transporters. Because there was less traffic going the other way we were able to bypass some of the broken or slower vehicles.

Driving was tricky. David did a good job without the shouting and cursing so typical of our previous driver. He had to drive very cautiously, always attempting to keep the left wheels on the asphalt road so the van would not become stuck in the soft sand like many similar vehicles. We often passed trucks and cars that had strayed into the dust and were resting in the soft sand, their wheels sunken and their drivers attempting to free them by pressing on the gas, which often got them deeper into the sand. Some crews worked hard to release their vehicles, sometimes assisted by tow trucks or armored personal carriers equipped with chains. When trucks filled with paratroopers passed us, David looked at them with intense and worried eyes, wondering if his son was among them.

Within a few kilometers our convoy blended with others, all heading west. Soon we lost sight of our battalion – even the messenger's jeep was not to be seen. I was unnerved, but comforted knowing that, since this was the only road west, we would eventually come across our battalion. I wished again that I had a way to communicate by a radio transmitter.

It seemed that the entire Israeli army was on the road. We progressed very slowly. After about ten kilometers we suddenly saw our battalion's messenger coming from the opposite direction. He had a message from our commanding officer.

"Some of our trucks were hit by artillery fire – there are casualties. You must try and get to the battalion's forward formation as quickly as possible."

He did not stay long enough for me to ask about the location of the casualties. Unfortunately, even if he had told me where they were, I did not have a map to assist in finding them. Spurred on by new urgency, we passed other vehicles as fast as we could. Because our van did not have a siren, let alone the markings of an ambulance, no one knew that we were actually serving as a medical transport. And due to the slow traffic in both directions, we made very little progress. Almost three hours after we received the message to reconnect with our battalion, we still had not reached them. As frustrating as this was, I realized that our convoy must have also been driving toward the canal, thus making it difficult for us to overtake them.

As we drove westward, we intermittently heard explosions of artillery shells in the distance. Overhead, Israeli jets streaked toward Egypt, making me feel safer, despite the blasts on the ground. After a while I noticed that the artillery shelling stopped whenever our jets were in the sky and resumed when they were gone. Apparently the presence of these jets posed a threat to the Egyptian artillery batteries and they held their fire until they left.

As we proceeded toward to the canal I felt as though we were getting deeper into the lion's den. We knew we were surrounded – the Egyptians were situated to the north, south and west; we traveled on a road wedged between the Second and Third Egyptian armies; and the Suez Canal was directly in front.

Chapter 13
In the Lion's Den

We were driving uphill when suddenly the traffic came to a standstill. Sounds of artillery were close but I could not see any explosions. They came from the direction of our road; however, the road was not visible to us from the bottom of the hill. Apparently the Egyptians had resumed their bombardment as soon as the Israeli jets stopped flying.

After waiting for a few minutes, I jumped out of the van and climbed to the top of the hill to see what had caused the delay. The sight was astounding and horrific at the same time. From the bluff where I stood, I saw that the road descended into a valley ahead. The valley was covered by numerous mushroom-like explosions that each artillery shell had created. As the shells fell, men ran away from the mass of vehicles crowding the road. I could see that vehicles with four wheel drive and armored personal carriers were steering away from the main road, seeking shelter in the surrounding hills south and north of the westward road. The trucks and vehicles that could not drive in the soft sand were stuck on the main road and their passengers were fleeing for cover.

Although I was standing only a kilometer away from this tableau, I paradoxically felt that we were safe from injury. It was a surreal sight which reminded me of a picture I had seen as a child in the Saturday Evening Post magazine depicting an ambushed American military convoy during the Second World War.

Beyond the shelling, I could see the Suez Canal and the Bitter Lake in the horizon. A cargo ship that had been there since the Six Day War was visible in the middle of the lake. To my surprise, Shmuel and Zvika, who had followed me to the top of the hill, urged me to keep on driving.

"We should keep driving forward so that we can join the battalion. That's where we're needed," Zvika said forcefully. "We got an order to get to the head of the convoy and we need to follow it."

It was clear to me at that minute that we could not go on; we needed to wait until the bombardment stopped and the road became passable again. Our van was particularly vulnerable because it had no protective armor. Furthermore, because it was not a four wheel drive, we could not drive off the road through the soft sand. I knew that, as long as the shelling continued, descending into the valley would be suicidal. I saw no reason to join the soldiers running for cover in the chaotic scene in the valley.

I realized that I was going to disobey an order, not a trivial matter in the army. However, unlike my medics, I gave priority to my common sense, according to what was feasible and safe at that time. If we were hit our regiment would lose all of its medical support. The order had been given several hours ago when the road was safer. Furthermore, without a radio, I could not reach our commanding officer or his staff to ask for their advice.

I felt uneasy about disobeying the order. *Can I do this? Can I make an independent decision and disregard an explicit order?* I recalled a famous legal case stemming from the 1956 Sinai Campaign. Several Israeli border policemen had been accused of killing Israeli Arab villagers from Kfar Kassem who had disobeyed a curfew. Apparently these farmers were returning from working in their field after dark, unaware that a curfew had been imposed on their village. The policemen argued in court that they had received orders to open fire on any person breaking the curfew, and as soldiers, were obligated to obey. The court found them guilty, holding that orders which are irrational or immoral should not be followed. This blind obedience to orders had also been the defense used by Nazis prosecuted for war crimes during the Nuremberg trials. It felt strange to think about Nazis logic to figure out what to do to preserve the lives of my medical team. But this legal precedent helped me decide to disobey the order and delay its execution until it would be safe to comply. I told myself that if I would ever be challenged, I would use that precedent to explain my actions.

Pressed again by Shmuel and Zvika to advance, I told them, "We're going to wait until the bombing ends. If we move now we'll be joining those people who are running for their lives away from their vehicles."

After about fifteen minutes we were joined at the top of the hill by a bus load of paratroopers who were part of a reserve battalion and looked to be in their early twenties. The soldiers dismounted their bus and we all watched the "Killing Valley" below. They were cheerful and in good spirits, even making jokes about the ongoing bombardment in front of us. They exuded a youthful energy and confidence and I wondered why they were in such great spirits despite the ominous situation. *Maybe it's their way of coping with the danger as a group. Jokes and laughter may, ironically, be the way that they can suppress their fears.*

David immediately approached them, asking whether they were part of his son's battalion. Learning that they were not, he said,

"I wish I could see my son, but I'm happy that he is not among them. They have intense fighting ahead of them. I just hope that wherever he is, he's safe."

I could sense the burden on his chest when he spoke.

Paradoxically, we felt safe at our viewing site. I figured that because we were further away from the canal than the valley ahead of us we were beyond the reach of Egyptian artillery. It was like watching a war movie and witnessing the helpless victims fleeing in all directions.

Suddenly everything changed. Shells began to fall on the hills north of us about half a kilometer away from where we stood. Clouds

113

of dust rose over the sand every time a shell hit the ground. Everyone's eyes were transfixed at the new bombardment site. It was suddenly clear that the enemy's artillery could reach us where we were standing and that we were no longer safe. After watching the shells for a minute, I realized that there was a pattern in the way the artillery shells were hitting the ground. They fell in a progressively eastward pattern about two hundred meters from each other. Based on my knowledge about how long range artillery is aimed and fired, it became clear that the shelling was done in a systematic way to calibrate the accuracy of the bombardment. Evidently, someone was trying to close in on us as well since we were stationed on a top of a hill that may have been visible to the enemy. Once the Egyptians calibrated their canons, it was only a matter of time before the shells would start falling on us.

Only later would I learn that an Egyptian artillery officer had been stationed on the abandoned cargo ship in the Bitter Lake and was directing enemy artillery fire at us very effectively. It took a direct hit by an Israeli jet on the ship to finally end the accurate shelling.

Once I realized that direct artillery fire was imminent, I told everyone to clear the ridge and return to the van. Since the road ahead of us was being shelled, the only safe direction was backward. Accordingly, I ordered our driver to turn around. We would back up from our elevated position and retreat some distance. We left the paratrooper bus behind and started to descend from the ridge; within a few minutes, we were again caught in a traffic jam, this time facing eastward, that brought us to a standstill. Suddenly, the situation became extremely dangerous as artillery shells started falling very close – about fifty meters north of the road. I looked around and realized that the vehicle adjacent to our van was a gasoline semi-trailer tanker carrying tons of fuel. If that vehicle would be hit, it would turn into a fireball, spilling its contents all around and changing the desert into an inferno of burning fuel. The resultant fire would engulf everything in a radius of at least a hundred meters.

Remaining with the van was not safe. In an instant, I ordered everyone to get out and run away. The best direction was away from the shells and toward the hills south of the road. I grabbed my Uzi and started running, not even taking any of the backpacks with medical supplies. Others were also running in the same direction. I realized that the farthest I distanced myself from the fuel loaded semi-trailer, the greater were my chances to survive if the vehicle was hit.

As I was running away, I became aware that I was doing exactly what my father had done thirty-five years earlier, three years before I was born, when the bus he was on was attacked by gunmen during the Arab revolt in Palestine in 1938. He never revealed to me what had happened to him but my mother told me the story. My father, who had been employed as a welder in the Shemen (oil) factory in Haifa, was riding the bus that took workers to the plant early in the morning. They had to pass through the Arab neighborhood of Wadi Rushmia. Just as the bus was crossing the narrow bridge over the deep valley that separated the Jewish and Arab portions of the town, heavy gun fire was opened on the bus.

The bus had no protective armor and the passengers were in grave danger of being hit. According to my mother, my father was the only one who jumped off the moving bus and ran toward the Jewish section of town. Apparently this action placed him at even greater danger because he was directly exposed to the bullets. Only the quick action of the bus driver and other passengers saved him from getting injured or killed. The driver backed up and my father's co-workers grabbed him and pulled him back onto the bus. Afterward, the driver was able to proceed away from the bridge; fortunately, none of the passengers was hurt. Apparently this experience was a very traumatic one for my father and he suffered from tremors for several months thereafter. Looking back, I realized that his symptoms, as detailed by my mother, bore a close resemblance to those associated with PTSD which, of course, was not recognized as such at that time.

After the Israeli War of Independence broke out in 1948, my father worked hard at placing improvised armor on public and military buses. These armored buses were called "Sandwiches" because their "armor" was comprised of a thick sheet of wood squeezed between two thin metal ones, an improvisation needed because of the scarcity of metal in the young country. Since Israel had no tanks or armored cars, the "Sandwich" buses became the backbone of public and military transportation. These vehicles protected supply convoys to the then-besieged city of Jerusalem, as well as travel between civilian centers.

I had been rather ashamed of my father's reaction and always hoped that I would react differently if I should ever be in a similar situation. My father died in 1966; I never talked to him about what had happened on that day in 1938 because I sensed that he was not eager to discuss it. Yet, as I was running away from the Egyptian shelling some thirty-five years later, I realized that I was reacting similarly; for the first time, I understood what my father might have felt when his bus was attacked. I was probably feeling the same fear of being a sitting duck; perhaps what he had done was the right thing to do under the circumstances. I hoped, however, that I was not running away because of panic as my father might have done.

To my surprise, running in the soft desert sand was not easy. Incredibly, we had never practiced that simple exercise in our formal training maneuvers. My feet were sinking in the sand and I made very little progress. After running for a few seconds my legs felt very heavy and every step I took required a tremendous effort. The Uzi, which weighed only three and a half kilograms, felt like it was three times heavier. I looked backward to the main road to gauge how far I had come and was disappointed to see that I was only about thirty meters away from the road. I was running for my life, but had not gone very far. For the first time in my life I realized that my chance of survival depended on my physical strength and stamina. I regretted that I was not in better shape so that I could distance myself even further away from the road. After realizing that I was making very little progress in the sand, out of breath and resigned to the surrounding risks, I finally gave up and stopped walking away from the road.

I looked around and saw that many other soldiers, all looking helpless, were as stuck as I was. Shells were still falling about a hundred meters north of the road and I hoped that the artillery fire would not spread to where we stood.

After about ten minutes the shelling stopped. Many of the soldiers began returning to their vehicles. My medics, my driver and I returned to find that our van was still stuck in traffic. We could not navigate out of the traffic jam by driving through the sand dunes because they were too soft and we would only sink. Many drivers had not yet returned to their abandoned vehicles and the road was a huge parking lot. Our goal of extracting the van was sidelined by the sounds of renewed artillery fire again landing around us. Having returned to the main road for only a few minutes, we sprinted back to the hills. Once more, I couldn't get very far because my legs sunk into the sand. It was inconceivable that we were all stuck. No one could stay long enough with their vehicles to untangle the congestion. And because of the numerous fuel and ammunition trucks all around, the situation grew even more perilous. It felt like we were caught next to a ticking bomb, just waiting for a match to fall from the sky.

Suddenly, help came from an unexpected source. I heared the voice of a man shouting over the sounds of the artillery explosions, "Everyone return to your vehicles right now! Get into them and let's drive away from here!"

I looked toward the sound of the voice and, to my amazement, saw a young lieutenant atop of the fuel tanker that had been parked next to our van. He stood only a hundred meters from the falling artillery shells as he urged everyone to ignore the enemy fire, return to their vehicles, and drive away. It was an amazing sight of a brave man who took the initiative and risked his life to save others. The sight of the lonely man disregarding enemy fire was so astounding that others imitated him, apparently overcoming their fear. Within a few minutes everyone obeyed the command and hesitantly returned to their vehicles. One by one, the vehicles moved away from the shelled area, directed by the brave lieutenant who stayed on top of the fuel tanker. This was happening despite the artillery barrage a short distance away. Since the driver of the fuel tanker next to us had not yet returned, the young lieutenant got into the driver's seat and drove it away, thus clearing a major obstacle.

Within minutes, the road was cleared and we were finally able to drive eastward, away from the dangerous area. What we had witnessed was a singular act of courage in which one person risked his life in order to take command of a confusing and dangerous situation and thus save the lives of many others. I felt that we owed our lives to the young officer for doing the right thing at a perilous time. While everyone else was running away, this man realized that leadership was needed so that lives would be spared and supplies would be saved. The dangerous situation created heroism. By standing on top of the potentially flammable fuel tank and ignoring the approaching artillery fire, he became a role model. I felt exceedingly grateful to the young officer whose name I never knew. I wished I could have related this incident to his commander so that he could have received a medal for his valor. I never found out what happened to him but, for me at least, he was one of the many unknown heroes who saved Israel.

Fortunately, none of the soldiers around us was seriously wounded. There were, however, several men who had suffered minor injuries from the bombardment. I saw two of them lying on the side of the road about 250 meters east of the area where we had been caught up in the shelling. We got out of our van to care for them. One had a minor injury on his hand and the other had injured his right eye. After examining the latter, I realized that he needed to be evacuated as soon as possible to save his eyesight. I suspected that his cornea was lacerated and he needed to be seen by a specialist. I gave him pain-reliving eye drops and bandaged his eye. I decided to take him to the Tassa military base since we were only about seven kilometers away.

Chapter 14
Temporary Reprieve

We arrived at the base as the sun was setting and the desert around us was becoming dark. The base lights were off and it took a while to find the medical clinic. The base, however, was humming with commotion. All manner of vehicles were moving around and soldiers were walking in all different directions. After getting instructions on how to find the clinic, we brought in the wounded soldier and made sure that he would be properly attended to. We then left the base in the direction of Akavish road to return to our battalion. It was getting hard to navigate in the darkness because most of the vehicles did not turn on their headlights so as to avoid detection by the enemy.

Arriving at the intersection leading to Akavish road, we were surprised to find it blocked by military police. No one was allowed to proceed because of heavy fighting and continuous bombardment along the road, and no one knew when it would be reopened. I realized that since all of our battalion's vehicles had already passed by, reuniting with our battalion during the night would be very difficult. I therefore decided to try and contact our commanding officer, inform him of our whereabouts, and get instructions on how to proceed. We drove back to Tassa base and found our way to the communication center located in an underground bunker.

This was a relatively large bunker with numerous radios and other communication equipment. The place was very noisy with personnel sitting at long tables wearing headphones and speaking loudly into microphones. The noise was deafening. I looked around and spotted a major who seemed to be in charge. I approached him and briefly outlined my predicament and why I had to contact my battalion. Initially reluctant to assist me, he said that everyone was too busy coordinating the fighting raging around us to help me. But knowing that my unit needed its medical team and ambulance, I insisted. Finally, the major relented and told one of the communications personnel to assist me.

It took about ten minutes for the young soldier to contact our battalion. The wireless connection was filled with static and the wireless link was very weak. I was able to assist the soldier in using his communication radio because I had some knowledge and experience with military communication methods and equipment. I had spent ten days in pre-military training in Gadna Kesher (Communication Youth Battalions) at the age of sixteen. Finally, that training had become useful.

At last I was able to speak with our deputy commanding officer who instructed me to stay in Tassa overnight and leave heading west early the next morning. Because of security concerns he could not tell me his location. He also did not know where the battalion would be in the morning, but assured me that we would have no trouble spotting it.

I conveyed my worry that in our absence there would be no medical support for the troops. He told me that our divisional medical support battalion had established a field hospital near our battalion's location and they could provide help if needed. Knowing that there was a field hospital near by was a relief to me. He reiterated that it would be best for us to stay put in Tassa because we might have trouble finding the battalion during the night.

In my rush to reunite with my battalion, I had unexpectedly been granted a reprieve from the fighting. As a result, we spent one night within the relative safety of a fenced-in military base. Nevertheless, memories from our previous experience at the Baluza military base taught me that even a seemingly secure base could be vulnerable to missile attacks.

I returned to the van to inform my medics about the news and was surprised to find one of the soldiers from the ammunition company standing with them. He had been brought over by Shmuel, who recognized him wandering on the base. The soldier was a thin man in his late twenties with no weapon or other military gear, including a helmet.

"He lost our battalion, so I brought him over" said Shmuel.

"What happened? How did you lose our battalion?" I asked the soldier.

"Our convoy was caught by heavy artillery fire and I ran into the hills along with everyone else. When the shelling stopped I decided not to return and just remained in the hills."

He answered in a hesitant voice, as if he were testing what my reaction would be.

Apparently he had been caught in the same road bombardment earlier that day.

"An armored troop carrier passed by the dunes where I was stranded and took me back to Tassa. I decided then that I just can't stand this war any more – I don't want to return to my unit. A few days ago I found out that my wife delivered a baby boy. I want to get out of this war alive so that I can see my newborn son. I'm afraid that if I go back to my unit I won't make it."

I was surprised by this man's honesty, and initially, had no idea how to respond. By that time, I had learned to accept soldiers' admissions of fear and I could appreciate what he had been through in the preceding hours. Like him, I had experienced a similar dread of dying as we ran away from our van. I learned through my past experience with Avner that it is impossible and probably wrong to force a soldier to return to unmanageable situations. I decided to allow the man to make his own choice of whether or not to return to his unit. He knew best what he was capable of handling. This approach was probably not in accordance with the policy of the military but, to me at least, it felt that it was the right one in that instance.

Finally, I told him, "I'm not going to report you as a deserter if you choose to leave but I'm leaving it up to you to decide if you want to return with us or go home. However, let me suggest that, if you want to be able to look into your son's eyes with pride as he grows up, I suggest that you return with us tomorrow morning."

I thought that this was the only argument I could use to convince him to return with us. Obviously, his newborn son was the main motivation for his decision. I thought that if he did not go back to his unit, his son might learn one day that his father had abandoned his duty out of fear. This was probably not the legacy this man wanted to leave his son.

He appeared to be surprised by my answer and did not respond. His eyes downcast, he left me and disappeared into the darkness. I had left the matter for the soldier to decide and wondered what would be his final choice.

The night we spent in Tassa was not restive. I slept inside the van and was awakened several times during the night by the sounds of heavy machine gun fire; apparently we had parked near an anti-aircraft machine gun position. I was started from deep sleep when I first heard the blasts. I instinctively grabbed my Uzi and jumped out of the van, not knowing what we were facing. Looking up, I could see tracer bullets lighting the sky. I suspected that the fire had erupted because of a suspicious object in the sky. Was it a missile, an enemy helicopter, an airplane? There was no one to ask. Once I realized the source of the noise, I tried to go back to sleep, although, my heart kept racing fast for several minutes. I never learned why fire had opened suddenly during that night and was too exhausted to ask. Even within a military base, I grew to accept the fragility of our situation.

We woke up early to join our battalion. When I got into the van I was glad to see the soldier who had contemplated desertion the night before. He got into the van as we were about to depart and sat quietly in the back seat. We did not exchange any words but booth of us knew that he had a difficult choice to make. I felt good about letting him make the decision without pressure. I thought that he had made the right choice for himself, one that he could live with.

Chapter 15
On the Banks of the Canal

Akavish road was open for traffic that morning as we retraced our way to our battalion. It was still heavily congested with buses, tank carriers, and supply trucks, as well as huge transports carrying parts of a floating bridge. Our van looked like a small fly sidling up to lumbering elephants, the larger military trucks. Our progress was slow even without needing to stop because of artillery fire. Although loudest in the east, the barrage of shelling could be heard from all directions. We learned from soldiers returning from the Canal that fighting was still going on north and south of the Akavish road but we were heartened that the skies above were controlled by Israeli jets.

We passed the place where we had abandoned the van and ran for cover and discovered several burned out trucks on the side of the road. It was evident that the enemy had finally hit vehicles in the road. *How lucky that we got out of that spot in time. If we would have stayed longer we could have ended up like these trucks,* I thought. *I hope those vehicles were empty when they were hit.*

We also passed the site where we had previously observed the shelling in the valley below us and found the skeleton of the bus that had carried the paratroopers who had stopped next to us the day before. Completely destroyed due to a direct artillery hit, its metal fragments and burned out tires lay by the side of the road. I prayed that none of its passengers had been killed or injured. However, since the explosion had happened almost sixteen hours earlier, there was no way to find out.

We continued driving, hoping to find our battalion among the numerous convoys that had been traveling with us or parked by the road side. After almost three hours, we finally recognized elements of our battalion waiting by the roadside and, within a few minutes, we located our command and control vehicles parked at a clearing along with several supply trucks. Many of the trucks in the division waited nearby. A few drivers and other soldiers lay next to the trucks, trying to nap. Their fatigue indicated that many of them had had a busy night. The silence of the encampment, intermittently broken by sporadic artillery fire, was eerie and unnerving.

The deputy commander was happy to see us. He had taken charge of the battalion on the previous night after our commanding officer left suddenly because he got word that his son was seriously injured during fighting on the Golan Heights. The deputy, previously over-shadowed by our active and forceful commanding officer, looked energized and in control. Now that he was in charge, I could see how well he performed in his position; he immediately instructed me to establish a site where I could care for any injured soldiers.

I learned from the deputy commanding officer that our battalion had reached the present location only a few hours earlier. We were less than a kilometer from the Suez Canal and were busy re-supplying the divisional tanks which were getting ready to cross the Canal into Egypt. We were expected to stay in this location for a while, at least until all the tanks and other combat elements could cross the bridge. I was told that the Egyptians had been shelling our area sporadically. One of our fuel trucks had sustained a direct hit earlier that morning and its two drivers who had been sitting in the cabin were killed instantly. "It was only a matter of time before the shells would strike again," he said in a matter-of-fact voice.

The idea that we would be crossing into Egypt was both exhilarating and scary. At last we were on the offensive and could teach the enemy a lesson that would not soon be forgotten. I was eager to see us avenge our losses and be part of the force that would carry the battle into Egyptian territory. At the same time, I felt a growing apprehension that, by crossing into Egypt, we would be at a greater risk of being cut off from the rest of the military. I thought about all the potential implications of this move. If our connection to Sinai was through a bridge or two, it would be difficult to get resupplied, evacuate wounded soldiers, or even retreat. I felt that we were about to go even deeper into the lion's mouth.

Looking around, I saw the tired and anxious faces of our soldiers. Most of them had experienced a sleepless night of driving and working, facing the constant fear of falling shells. Many of them wore frozen expressionless demeanors. I imagined how they were coping with the experience of being forced to stay in one place while they faced relentless enemy fire. It must have been like standing in front of a firing squad, never knowing when the hour of execution would arrive. The priority was to allow tanks and armored personal carrier units to cross the newly established bridge over the Canal while the supply battalion waited for them to complete their crossing. Unfortunately, while we were waiting, we were an easy target.

I instructed my medics to take their personal shovels and start digging their own foxholes. We all knew how to dig foxholes in the ground; now was the time to seek cover. We always carried shovels throughout our various training exercises but had never before used them. Suddenly, our lives depended on these simple one foot trowels, but the task of digging was very difficult. In contrast to the soft sand we had encountered a day earlier, this soil was very hard and felt like dried up cement. I assumed that exposure to salty water from the Canal and Bitter Lake must have hardened the desert sand over the years. After a few frustrating minutes, we realized that we could not effectively dig holes in the soil. The constant barrage of shells falling not far away reminded us that we need to find a shelter for the van, which contained our medical materials, as soon as possible. It became clear that if we stayed above ground we were likely to be hit.

Fortunately, I spotted a bulldozer busy digging trenches not far away and asked the operator to help us secure a ditch large enough to hide our van so that we could treat and hold any injured soldiers. The bulldozer operator immediately agreed to help, recognizing the importance of shielding the medical unit. As he dug into the hard sand, creating a secure place for us, I prayed that he would finish the job before the next artillery salvo hit. It was a strange sensation to feel that our lives depended on the speed and performance of a piece of equipment, a larger version of the shovels we all carried. Even though the process of digging the large trench took only about fifteen minutes, it felt like an eternity.

I felt a great sense of relief to finally see the trench completed. It was an inclined trench with a downward slope that could only protected part of the vehicle – not exactly perfect protection, but better than nothing. David rolled the van backward into the trench so that only the front was exposed. Having a secure location would allow us to treat injured soldiers with a greater degree of safety. We then unloaded a container of medical equipment and placed it behind the van. We had to work in a very tight space behind the rear of the van and the wall of sand at the bottom of the trench.

From time to time I ordered the driver to move the van out of the shelter and drive to bring in newly injured soldiers. Although he promptly complied without hesitation, I could sense his relief when he rolled the van back into the safety of the trench. A medic was also needed on these trips and Shmuel and Zvika always volunteered. They were unfailingly enthusiastic in this capacity, and I had to remind them on each trip to be careful and avoid taking unnecessary risks.

We became oblivious to the sound of explosions. After a barrage of artillery fell close by, a jeep pulled up to the van, the driver shouting in our direction:

"Come quickly. Several soldiers have been hit by an explosion."

Although I did not want to leave our position, which by now had become an unofficial first aid station, it seemed prudent to get to the injured soldiers as soon as possible. We quickly placed our medical supply container back into the van and pulled out of the trench.

As we followed the jeep I saw how vulnerable our battalion was. Ammunition and fuel trucks were parked along the narrow road with their crews sitting in their shadows or inside the cabins. These trucks contained highly dangerous materials and, if hit, could explode and kill or severely wound these men. An eerie testament to the vulnerability of these vehicles was the burned - out trucks we observed on our drive. There was, unfortunately, no alternative to this dangerous situation; these trucks were the lifeline of the fighting forces.

Within ten minutes we arrived at the explosion site. About fifty meters from the road we observed three injured men lying next to a small crater in the sand, its center and bushes around it were burned out. I quickly examined the three soldiers who were already being assisted by their friends. One of the injured had sustained multiple shrapnel wounds in his back, was coughing out blood, and had some breathing difficulty. The other two had second degree burns in their hands and chests.

It was obvious that the first man was the one who needed immediate care. I was concerned that the shrapnel had created a pneumothorax (perforation of the lungs), potentially a deadly injury. Since it was difficult to perform a through examination in the midst of the field, I decided to prevent the development of a pneumothorax by sealing the shrapnel's penetration sites in the back with a sheets of plastic. Although I had never done this before, I had seen it being done by others in the emergency department in Hadassah Medical Center. I was fortunate to have worked there as nurse during the last two years of my medical school education and had gained significant experience in acute care and trauma – an extremely useful skill at the moment.

Although we had not practiced this procedure before, my medics knew exactly how to assist me in sealing the wounds and we did not need to exchange many words before the soldier received his treatment. Zvika delivered oxygen from a small oxygen tank, and Ehud taped the plastic tight around the wounds. Within a few minutes of our arrival we were able to place the three wounded soldiers in our van and, while driving to the nearest field hospital, we were able to attend to the less seriously wounded. We were fortunate to reach our destination within a few minutes because our driver, David, knew the location from his earlier trips.

I immediately informed the surgeon at the hospital about the condition of each of our patients. It was difficult for me to let others take over for the care of the most seriously wounded man. As a physician, I felt responsible for him and wanted to continue my care. I knew, however, that I was passing the torch to a better equipped and better trained team and by doing so as swiftly as possible I was actually increasing his odds of survival.

As I watched the hospital team I was reminded by Zvika that we had no more time to linger, as our battalion needed us. *He was right again,* I thought. *Who knows what's waiting for us at the first aid station. There may be more wounded soldiers there.*

We quickly returned to our battalion and rolled the van back into its shelter. Happily, there were no new wounded men waiting for us. The whole trip took less than an hour —yet it felt much longer. We had our first test of dealing with a multiple injury situation and made a difference in saving a person's life.

Over the afternoon we took care of about thirty individuals who had been injured or who had become ill. Most had superficial lacerations or injured joints; some had burns and shrapnel wounds. I had to evacuate only two with more serious wounds. One had a fracture of the leg and the other had shrapnel wound in his abdomen.

As we were caring for the soldiers, I reminded the medics to document the treatment and medications we gave each individual on cards that we attached to their uniforms. This was what we were taught to do so that future medical teams would know the diagnosis and treatment, thus preventing errors, including over-medicating with narcotics. For the first time during the war, our medical unit was treating people under fire and I was relieved that we seemed to be functioning very smoothly. A handful of soldiers asked for anti-anxiety medications; I spent some time talking with each of them.

One of them described his experiences from earlier that day when he had been refueling tanks about to cross into Egypt. He had been busy working in an open area just opposite the bridge over the Canal when a sudden salvo of shells landed in the area. A gasoline truck near him had caught on fire with the drivers still sitting in their seats. He had tried to open the cabin doors but the intense fire and heat prevented him from helping the drivers inside. He was helpless as he watched them burn. His hands were still shaking and he had tears in his eyes when he told me the story. It was the first time I had seen a soldier actually break down and cry and it was very difficult to hide my own tears.

As the hours passed, our situation became more and more unnerving. The general quiet was intermittently interrupted by jets flying overhead and sounds of artillery. About every half an hour we were hit by a barrage of artillery fire as Katyusha rocket shells exploded in the dunes around us. I jokingly called that kind of shelling a "Slow Drip," a reference to how intravenous fluids flowed into the veins, drop after drop. The medics found this description funny and adopted it. The shelling was not enough to cause substantial damage, but it was certainly disquieting and constantly interrupted our activities. I assumed that the Egyptians refrained from continuously firing to avoid being spotted by Israeli fighter jets in the area.

Chapter 16
My Luck Ran Out

It was late in the afternoon and the sun was far down in the west. After an hour of relative quiet and having no more sick individuals to care for, I decided to walk among the battalion's scattered trucks. I thought that in this way I could spot soldiers too busy to see me or who did not know how to find us. I also thought I could lift the spirits of our men, hoping that by seeing me they would feel better knowing that I was around should they need me. I woke up Ehud, the head medic, who had been napping in the driver's seat and told him of my plans. I promised to be back in less than an hour.

As I put my helmet over my head, I purposefully ignored the chin strap. I had read that fastening the helmet's strap could lead to an injury if a blast occurs nearby. The force of an explosion could sheer the helmet off the head and the belt could traumatize the chin. Even though I was not sure that this was accurate, I always followed this custom as did most soldiers. I never questioned this practice, but I felt reassured that this was the right thing to do by watching Hollywood war movies where most of the actors wore their helmets in a similar fashion.

Helmets had a special significance to me in war. I remembered how a helmet nearly cost me my life right after the Six Day War. It was five days after the fighting was over and I was still in uniform. Since the flow of casualties to Hadassah Medical Center's emergency room had finally ended, I was given a couple of days off. My friend

Rami, who had come home to Jerusalem for a short liberty from his unit in the Golan Heights, suggested that I join him on the way back to his unit and explore the newly captured West Bank and Golan Heights. I was thrilled to have the opportunity to discover the newly captured territories. I had lived in Jerusalem for eight years and felt confined by the border encircling the city from the north, east, and south. The West Bank, known as "Gada," was so close but also very far. I finally had the opportunity to see first hand what lay beyond the old border.

We hitchhiked on the road from Jerusalem to the town of Jericho on the west bank of the Jordan River and were fortunate to hop on a military command car headed in that direction. To our surprise, the entire area east of Jerusalem was a desert. I felt a special sense of discovery and elation, as I felt connected to the land because of its ancient biblical history. The driver stopped halfway to Jericho to view the spectacular monasteries built on the cliffs of Wadi (dry river bed in Arabic) Kelt. The view was breathtaking and we decided to descend on foot into the wadi.

Once we arrived at the bottom of the path, I took a walk upstream along the dry river. Although I knew that walking in the deserted wadi by myself might not be very wise, I felt an invulnerability enhanced by the intoxication of the recent unforeseen victory over our enemies. After a short walk I arrived at a deserted fortified Jordanian army bunker. It was a small round concrete post with an iron door in the rear and small slits of windows that protected the interior from enemy fire while allowing the inhabitants to shoot at an approaching adversary.

The door was partially open and I carefully walked inside. It was very dark and musty and I was relieved to find it deserted. After a couple of minutes my eyes adjusted to the darkness and, to my surprise, I saw a Jordanian army helmet lying on the floor. It was camouflaged and covered with a thin net, like a fisherman's discarded catch. From my rented room in Jerusalem on the border of the city, I had seen these helmets on the heads of Jordanian soldiers walking along the walls of the Old City of Jerusalem only a few hundred yards away. It must have been left by a fleeing soldier escaping the West Bank on his way back to the east bank of the Jordan River.

Wow, I thought, *this helmet would be a great souvenir!*

In retrospect, I should have never touched the helmet. We had been warned not to pick up any left over "souvenirs" because they might be booby-trapped. Several Israeli soldiers had been seriously injured by such innocent looking items. I could not, however, resist the temptation. As a precaution, I pushed the helmet with a stick and nothing happened. I picked it up and walked back down the river carrying it in my right hand. Suddenly, my ears filled with shouts in Arabic and Hebrew: "Kif" ("stop" in Arabic) "Atzor" ("stop" in Hebrew)!!"

I could see a group of soldiers a few hundred meters away aiming their rifles at me. From their uniforms and the fact that they spoke Hebrew, I knew they were Israeli. But did they know who I was? I shouted back to them, identifying myself as an Israeli. When I finally reached them they told me that from a distance I looked like a Jordanian soldier holding his helmet. This danger had never occurred to me when I picked up the helmet. The Israelis said that they had me in the sights, and were ready to shoot at me. Fortunately, they waited until I got closer and could respond. My wish to keep that helmet nearly cost me my life.

The memories of the purloined Jordanian helmet disappeared as I emerged from our trench near the Suez Canal. The safety of our impromptu bunker was gone and I had only my own helmet to protect me. I took a shortcut, walking over the sand dunes toward a group of trucks parked further down the road. In a flash, I found myself on my side in the sand. I had no idea how I got to be in that position. I felt a sharp pain in my left leg and on the left side of my face. Blood gushed through my torn trousers. I put my hands on my face but it seemed as though there was no injury. My helmet was still on. I noticed a small crater in the sand about fifteen meters away that, in retrospect, must have been the place where an artillery shell or Katyusha rocket must have fallen. *I've been hit!*, I thought, but *I'm still alive and I don't think I'm badly injured. Wow, I'm really lucky.*

I must have lost consciousness for a few minutes. My mind was cloudy but I could feel an excruciating pain in my left leg. *The explosion must have pushed me to the ground and my helmet must have protected me when my head hit the ground.* I tried to stand up, but the pain in my leg intensified. I inspected my bleeding leg and realized that I had a small penetrating wound. It was a sight that had become familiar in the past ten hours. About three centimeters long with irregular margins, the gash was typical of a Katyusha rocket shrapnel. *The shrapnel must be buried inside my leg; I'm really lucky to have survived.*

I let the wound bleed for a while so that the blood would wash away the sand. I always carried in my shirt pocket a few self-injectable morphine ampoules and a first aid bandage in case I needed them in an emergency. I injected myself with an ampoule of morphine and poured some water from my canteen over the wound. I then placed a bandage over the wound and waited for the pain killer to take effect. Fortunately, my pain subsided after a few minutes and I was able to stagger back to our encampment. My Uzi, which had never left my side, felt very heavy as I approached our van.

My medics were alarmed when they saw me. Ehud took off my bandage, cleaned my wound with an antiseptic solution, and reapplied a new bandage. I told my men what had happened. Shmuel reacted by telling me:

"Doc, you must say the Gomel prayer when this is over. You could have been killed".

I nodded my head and promised to go to the synagogue and stand before the ark to recite the prayer thanking God for sparing my life. After I survived a motorcycle accident years earlier, my father reminded me to recite that prayer. I did so then and again after surviving the Six Day War.

I reassured my medics that I had only a minor injury and that I was otherwise fine. *I need to convince them that I'm OK,* I thought. *They all need me to care for our battalion. I can't let my small injury stand in the way.* I also knew that, even though the shrapnel might be still in my leg, the worst was over since the bleeding had stopped. Fortunately, I had no loss of sensation or movement and the arteries in my foot were palpable, meaning that no essential structure had been injured. *Besides, most shrapnel wounds are left alone so I don't need any further treatment. In the great scheme of things, I'm lucky to have survived with so little injury.*

What I had not realized in those moments was that I was rejecting the fact that I had indeed been hurt. Also, for the first time in my life, I was under the influence of a powerful narcotic that not only masked my pain but also interfered with my judgment. The drug had cloaked the sense of worry and fear which had protected me during the past few days.

My recollection of the events over the next ten hours is hazy, and I was able to nap only for short intervals through the night. I remember that we were called several times to drive out of our trench during the night to care for wounded soldiers along the road, as well as to the loading area, dubbed "the Yard," near the pontoon bridge over the Canal. This was the name given to the area that was the embarkation point for tanks and other vehicles to cross the canal. Tanks, armored personal carriers, trucks, and other vehicles passed through the Yard on the way to Egypt. Crews would wait there until the newly constructed military bridge was available for them to pass.

The area was constantly in motion except when fired upon. Although the Yard looked chaotic, there was an inherent order in the commotion. Men shouted at each other, straining their voices to overcome the sounds of the engines and artillery fire, as they issued directions and instructions on how and where to drive their vehicles. Drivers and tank crews prepared their vehicles to cross the bridge by fastening their ropes and placing their equipment in secure places.

While we stopped at the Yard, I took care of injured truck drivers and other personnel. We would load them into our van and drive them to the field hospital nearby. On several occasions, we encountered enemy artillery fire that seemed as close as before. But this time, because of the darkness, and also perhaps because of my inability to judge risk, I ignored it. It seemed to me that I had passed beyond the barrier of fear and felt invulnerable. I don't know if it was the narcotics or the hum of activity, but I found that it was easier for me to ignore my fear on that night. In the midst of it all, I was in a constant state of movement as I was needed by so many people.

All night we drove back and forth from the yard to the field hospital. When the sun finally rose at five in the morning I noticed that I could not tolerate the light striking my left eye and was forced to use my hand as a makeshift eye patch. I checked my eye in the driver's side mirror and, to my astonishment, my left pupil was fixed in a completely dilated position and there was a bluish discoloration in the skin of my left eye socket. On the other hand, the right pupil reacted normally to light and constricted when I flashed light on it. *This is strange,* I thought. *I didn't know that I injured my eye.* As the effects of the morphine began to fade, I started to feel some pain in my left check. *Could this one-sided dilation of the pupil be a sign of an intracranial bleed?* I asked myself. Trauma to the head can cause fatal bleeding into the brain or its envelopes. I was, of course, concerned, but before I had time think about it, a new problem arose.

David, our driver, started to complain of difficulty in breathing and pain in his left chest. Since he was older than any of us, I was concerned that he was at risk of a heart attack. I suspected that our strenuous and dangerous missions during the previous night might have caused his symptoms and I decided to have him evaluated at the nearby field hospital.

Although we had been at the hospital several times during the night, it was only in the daylight that I could appreciate its size. Comprised of several huge camouflaged tents staffed by physicians, including surgeons, internists, an otolaryngologist, and even a neurosurgeon it contained a triage area, a small operating room, as well as treatment and holding areas. Several wounded soldiers lay on stretchers waiting to be evacuated by helicopter.

While David was being evaluated I asked one of the surgeons whom I had seen several times the night before to examine me. He looked exhausted after a sleepless night. I told him about my injury and how I had treated my leg wound. I also shared with him my recent new eye findings.

"Why didn't you tell me that you had been injured earlier?" he inquired angrily.

"I was too busy taking care of the wounded, and I didn't think my injuries were very serious," I replied.

He proceeded to examine me and called the neurosurgeon on staff to also evaluate me.

The neurosurgeon conveyed his conclusions in a concise and determined voice:

"You're right that your leg wound is small. However, I'm concerned about your head injury. The one sided dilatation of the left pupil may be related to that injury, and as you well know, this may be an ominous sign of intracranial bleed. You have to be evacuated right away in case your condition deteriorates."

While I didn't want to believe this grim assessment, I couldn't argue with the doctor's impartial appraisal of my condition. Still, I didn't believe that I actually had a bleed inside my brain. Although I had cared for patients with intracranial bleeds in the past, by the time I saw them they were generally in bad shape. I had never seen anyone at an earlier stage of such a bleed. Could I be at the beginning of this fatal process?

"I can't leave my soldiers now," I protested but my argument fell on deaf ears.

"You have to be evacuated right away. If your condition deteriorates there's little we can do to help you here."

On instructions of the surgeon, a medic placed a bandage over my left eye, thus relieving the annoying overexposure to light. He also changed the bandage over my wounded leg and quickly prepared the paperwork related to my evacuation.

I was shaken by the sudden decision to be evacuated. When I approached the surgeon, I was totally unprepared for this eventuality. Reluctant to leave the war zone, I had struggled with my fears throughout the war and now that I had finally mastered them, I had to leave. I had been able to perform well throughout a most difficult day despite my fear, and in the end, had even become oblivious to its existence. Now that I was finally ready and capable of dealing with it, I was being forced to leave. I also felt a tremendous obligation to my battalion. After the previous night's tough moments, I couldn't leave these soldiers when medical help was desperately needed, even more than before. Yet, as physician, I knew I couldn't argue with the logic of the doctors' assessment.

"Who will care for my battalion if I leave?"

"Don't worry, someone will replace you," answered the surgeon.

As we were talking I heard the sounds of helicopter rotors above.

A large cargo Sikorsky helicopter was descending in a cloud of dust and landed in a large yard across from the hospital's tents.

"Hurry up!" the physician shouted inside the helicopter, "We need to load everyone quickly so that we can take off before the shells hit!"

I immediately recognized the physician; it was Achikam Avni (Feinstein), my classmate in medical school. We had finished medical officers' course together four years ago and I had not seen him since. Always a model officer, he had been chosen the outstanding graduate of that course. Clearly, he was thriving as a medical officer in the air force, evacuating wounded soldiers. Even though we were in the midst of the war, Avni's uniform was immaculately ironed.

It was a strange coincidence to see him. Too busy to come over as he familiarized himself with the conditions of the wounded soldiers, we waved to each other. I didn't need active treatment during the flight as did so many others. I remembered from our officers' course how essential it was to stabilize the condition of any evacuee prior to transportation because manipulations and instrumentations are very difficult inside a vibrating helicopter. Avni was occupied doing his job, ensuring that all the injured were ready to be transported.

Within minutes, the medics loaded the helicopter with wounded soldiers on stretchers. Many were receiving intravenous fluid or blood. I recognized one of the incapacitated soldiers as someone from my battalion, whom I had treated only a few of hours earlier. The two in-flight medics made sure that all the wounded had their intravenous fluids set properly. Everyone had individual cards on his chest listing all the medications and treatment he had received. I felt strange to be among so many wounded soldiers without having a role in their care. I suddenly became a patient – defrocked from my position as a physician.

Several of the wounded with minor injuries were able to climb up the helicopter's ramp by themselves. Our driver, David, was among the evacuees. He was lying on a stretcher receiving oxygen. Apparently the doctors felt that his condition merited evacuation. I went over to him and shook his hand, assuring him that he would be fine.

I had little time to say goodbye to Ehud, my head medic. I left him my Uzi and its ammunition cartridges, knowing that my weapon would serve him better than his old rifle. I mumbled a few parting words and apologized for leaving him and the rest of our medical team. He assured me that things would be all right and he promised to take charge of everything until my replacement arrived. He also told me that he would try to find me later to update me about the whereabouts of our battalion. Finally, he promised to bring me all my personal articles that I had left behind. Truthfully, I didn't know if I would ever see him again. I shook his hand and walked unsteadily onto the helicopter.

Chapter 17
Evacuation

The helicopter was packed with about twenty-five stretchers suspended in sets of three on each side of the cabin. Avni and the medics on board were busy attending to the wounded, adjusting their intravenous fluids lines, making sure that they were comfortable on their stretchers, and administering pain relieving medication. One man, more gravely injured than the rest, was artificially ventilated by one of the medics. I took a seat with other less seriously wounded soldiers on a small cloth bench and waited for the helicopter to take off.

Within thirty seconds the huge helicopter rose up in a cloud of dust flying low between the hills to avoid detection by the Egyptians. For a few seconds I could see the Suez Canal and our clustered forces around it. Soon the familiar scene that I had been a part of disappeared. The battlefield was left behind. After a short distance the helicopter gained more altitude and proceeded eastward. It felt good to fly away from the war zone because our risk of being shot down diminished. With each meter of elevation, my anxiety over the last twelve days diminished. This was a unique sensation of relief that I had never felt before in my life. I was abruptly being extracted from hell.

Yet my relief was tinged with guilt. On the one hand, I was grateful to this great aircraft for lifting me from the killing grounds. I was no longer in an imminent threat of being shot at, ambushed, or attacked from the air. On the other hand, I felt bad that I was out of danger while my medics and the other soldiers were still exposed to threats, which were greater then than ever before. Worst of all, my battalion had to face these dangers without its physician. This realization weighed heavily on my chest and, in the end, outweighed the sense of relief.

Once we attained a steady flying speed I got out of my seat to assist Avni and his medics in attending to the wounded. I was not asked to do this, but reacted spontaneously because the two medics on board could not handle all the work. Even though my bandaged left eye made it difficult to balance I checked on the intravenous infusions of those close to me and made sure that they were flowing well. I also fixed their bandages and assisted them as needed. Apparently the vibrations of the helicopter had loosened some of the bandages and changed the speed of the infusions. I felt glad to be able to be of some assistance and able to use my medical skills. For a few moments I could forget my pain and the fact that I was also wounded.

The sounds of the engines were deafening and the medics and Avni worked silently. They wore ear muffs as protection from the noise, making it difficult to communicate. However, they seemed to know what to do without uttering many words and used hand signs to communicate with each others. Occasionally, they shouted in the ears of the wounded soldiers so that they could be heard. I could see that all the wounded were stoically bearing their pain and discomfort. There was no moaning or sounds from anyone on board. We were silent. No one complained.

Even though the noise was deafening and he had to lift his ear muffs to be able to hear me, I had a chance to communicate a little with Avni by shouting into his ears. He told me that he had been flying numerous evacuation missions since the war had started and that his helicopter had been shot at several times. Surprisingly, he did not look tired or worn out, but was full of energy as he constantly paced back and forth through the helicopter.

Our flight only lasted half an hour. We landed at Refidim (Bir Gafgafa), a large military base about seventy kilometers east of the

Suez Canal. Waiting for us at the landing site were a row of military ambulances with their engines running. The wounded were unloaded one by one into the waiting ambulances. I bid goodbye to Avni and boarded one of the ambulances, not knowing that this would be the last time I would see him. Avni was killed six months later on the slopes of Mount Hermon in the Golan Heights, three weeks after he got married. He was doing his everyday job, evacuating wounded soldiers, during an intense fire fight with the Syrians. Even though the war had ended by that time, the Syrians had been intermittently shelling the Israeli forces in the Golan Heights. A direct hit by a mortar shell killed him instantly, along with a wounded soldier he was helping. He was one of seven physicians killed during the Yom Kippur War and the months that followed. During that period thirty-five physicians were wounded. Unlike other wars, physicians were supporting troops as close to the fighting as possible. This resulted in a high casualty rate among physicians, who had usually been spared from such high fatality rates.

From inside the ambulance, I saw the helicopter take off again within moments of discharging its last passenger on its way to another evacuation mission. Unlike Tassa and Baluza, the base on which we landed was very large with numerous buildings and installations spread over the flat desert terrain. I was taken to a large field hospital made up of several large open tents with about forty field beds each. Most of the beds were empty and, surprisingly, there were only about a dozen other wounded soldiers in them. Even though I was surrounded by wounded men, I immediately sensed that this hospital environment was calmer than those located in the midst of battle. The relative lack of a military threat relaxed the base inhabitants. It felt good to have a reprieve from the constant commotion and tension that I had experienced in the last several days.

I was quickly seen by several doctors who examined me, performed radiographs of my skull and face, and inspected my eyes. Relieved to learn that I did not have a skull fracture, I still needed to be shipped to a hospital even farther to the rear where my left eye could be examined by a specialist. The doctors suspected that I might have fractured one of my facial bones, although the radiological equipment in the field hospital was not sophisticated enough to investigate this type of subtle fracture. Because my condition was relatively stable and because I did not exhibit any signs of active intracranial bleeding, it was decided not to ship me right away but to keep me overnight. The plan was to evacuate me the next day in an airplane along with other less seriously wounded soldiers. All the empty spaces on the planes that day were saved for more seriously injured soldiers.

Although I was happy to hear the physicians' opinion, I was still concerned about my eye and kept taking the bandage off to see if my pupil was still dilated. During the ensuing hours a swelling had developed around my left eye and my left pupil stayed fixed in its position. I was hoping that the emergence of swelling around the eye suggested that my injury was limited to that area only. I was reassured by the fact that I was feeling well and did not develop any signs of bleeding into the brain.

I was finally able to shave and take a shower after twelve days and put on new underwear and socks. Noticing that these amenities had been donated by Jewish American organizations made me feel good and made me realize that we were not alone in our struggle.

One of the first things I wanted to do was to call my wife and let her know that I was safe. The hospital had special phone booths for soldiers to call home. I was able to reach my wife and let her know what had happened. I did it calmly and carefully so as not to alarm her. I underplayed the nature of my injuries and told her that I would let her know which hospital I would be admitted to. Although she had been getting along fine without me, she was relieved to hear from me. She reported that everyone in the building had to spend several nights in the shelter during the first few days of the war and also let me know of a tragedy that had struck our neighbors who lived a floor below us. Their twenty-eight year old son, a reserve paratrooper, was killed the fighting at the Chinese Farm. I was shaken to hear this. Although I did not know the young man well, I sensed that the war had finally affected the safest area of my life: my peaceful apartment building in Rehovot. Now two families from the same building were affected. I was afraid that once I returned home I would hear even more bad news about friends and family members who would be irreparably damaged in this war.

Taking care of wounded soldiers myself and observing so many injured in the field clinic over the past days had given me a distorted view of the war. I saw the most grim and depressing side of battle. The endless number of casualties made the human cost of the war very high in my mind. I had a similar experience during the Six Day War when I worked in the Hadassah Hospital emergency room. Over a three day period, I saw hundreds of casualties. I felt at that moment as I did then: very sad and despondent.

Even though Israel lost over six hundred soldiers in the Six Day War, that conflict resulted in a victory which increased the security of the country. On the other hand, the current war seemed futile and unnecessary. Israel had nothing to gain from it. This time we fought for our survival. What was painful to me was the realization that, this time, many of the casualties could have been avoided. I saw how soldiers had fallen because we were unprepared to fight a war and how lives were lost because we lacked essential equipment, supplies, and manpower.

I was finally able to lie down and sleep after a nearly sleepless night before. Finally, I could rest my body. Yet my mind was still racing. My thoughts were with my medics and my battalion. Even though I realized that my injuries had to be treated, I kept feeling guilty that I had left my comrades.

Among the doctors I observed caring for the injured I suddenly recognized Michael Kuhn, a medical school classmate who had left Israel to do a psychiatry residency in New York City. I had not seen him since our graduation five years earlier. It seemed as if this war was some kind of morbid class reunion. Like everyone else, he was wearing an Israeli army uniform. But because he had been away from Israel for several years, he had not taken a medical officer course and therefore had no military ranks on his shoulders. He had just arrived from the States to assist in patient care. He told me that as soon as the war broke out he had contacted the Israeli Consulate in New York who sent him and other reserve soldiers back to Israel. We were very glad to see each other and I told him about my recent injury.

Michael informed me that he was busy caring for soldiers who were suffering from what he called "Post Traumatic Stress Disorder" (PTSD). This was a completely new phrase for me. Although I had seen many individuals who had exhibited stress over the past two weeks, I was ill prepared to deal with it.

I had the misconception that anyone evacuated from the battle because of psychological stress reaction to his combat experience should not be allowed to return to the war zone. In my opinion stressful reaction proved that the soldier was unfit for combat. But what I saw Michael do was entirely the opposite. Seeing how Michael treated his patients opened my eyes to the best way of helping individuals with PTSD.

I followed Michael as he walked over to a soldier sitting on the edge of a field bed. He looked drawn and depressed; he was unshaven and his uniform was dusty and charred. When Michael spoke to him, he stared at the floor. Yet Michael encouraged the soldier to talk about what had happened to him. To my surprise, he wanted him to relive his traumatic experiences. The twenty-six year old reserve tank commander was initially resistant to share his story. After some time, however, he started to slowly describe his last battle. He related that his tank had been hit by a Sagar hand-held missile. All the members of his crew were instantly killed, but he somehow managed to jump out of the burning tank and watch helplessly while his friends burned inside the tank. He had served with those men for seven years. In that instant, he said, his whole world fell apart. Once he escaped from the tank he encountered intense enemy fire that kept him pinned down behind a hill until he was finally rescued. His body was shaking as he recounted his story. It was clear that it was very difficult for him to talk about what he had experienced.

Michael listed attentively to the man and kept encouraging him to tell us everything. His tone of voice conveyed empathy and understanding. After the man finished his story, Michael hugged him. It was evident that the soldier seemed to have benefited from the opportunity to talk to us. Even though the examination took place in the middle of a busy hospital tent, the intensity of the dialogue created an intimate exchange.

I was sure that Michael would recommend evacuating the soldier to the center of Israel, perhaps to be cared for at a large medical facility. To my surprise, his treatment plan was entirely different. Michael told the patient that he would be allowed to rest for a couple of days away from the raging battle and then return to his unit. During that period of respite he would get a new military uniform to replace his charred one, take showers, call home, and have decent meals. Again, I was surprised – the soldier willingly accepted the plan; although traumatized, he was content with the news that he would return to his unit.

I could not believe that Michael's plan was to return this mentally traumatized soldier to the front lines. Later, however, Michael explained to me that this was the current standard of care for PTSD victims and was based on the experience of American forces in Vietnam. The Americans had learned that returning patients to their previous duties after a short respite worked much better than sending them away. Prohibiting soldiers from being with their units branded them as psychological casualties. A similar practice was also apparently in effect in the Israeli Air Force; a pilot who had crashed his plane was encouraged to fly again as soon as possible so that he would not lose his self confidence. According to Michael, this plan, which still seemed strange to me, had worked numerous times in the past. He was confident that it would most likely work with this soldier.

I accepted him at his word and realized that I had learned something important that I wished I had known earlier. I could have used this technique with some of my soldiers, including my medic Avner. I had delayed evacuating several men because I was afraid that they would never return to the battlefield. I didn't want them to live with the stigma of knowing that they had fallen apart under pressure. This attitude was the product of the macho culture in Israel that did not acknowledge or encourage talking about weakness. What Michael showed me was that it was possible to assist soldiers with PTSD. If reached and treated early enough before they fell apart, they could eventually return to their comrades.

What I had learned from Michael supported what I found out myself about how to deal with fear. It is better to admit it, accept it as a normal feeling, and talk openly about it. Avoiding and hiding it are detrimental. I had seen this work in my soldiers. When they were encouraged to speak openly about their anxieties and fears and when they saw me accept their emotions as normal reactions to danger, most were able to return to their duties.

Chapter 18
In the Hospital

Early the next morning, I was driven by ambulance to the airstrip along with several other medical evacuees. We boarded a two-propeller cargo plane and took off toward the north. In contrast to the helicopter flight of a day earlier, the patients on this plane were medically more stable. Some sat on regular seats, as I did, and did not need much care during the flight. However, several of them were lying on stretchers and required intravenous fluids. We were accompanied by a physician and three medics. This time I did not feel the need to assist them. Yet I still felt strange, as I never expected to return from the war by plane.

As we took off, I looked out the window at the direction of the Suez Canal where the war was still raging, hoping to see the battlefield and perhaps get an idea of what was going on. To my disappointment, the visibility was poor because of the morning haze. I worried about my battalion, hoping that they had already received a physician to replace me. Many questions ran through my mind: Had they already crossed into Egypt? Did we sustain more casualties? Are all the medics okay?

As the plane approached the southern part of Israel, I started to see green fields and settlements. Within a short time I observed the city of Tel Aviv and, in the horizon, I could observe my hometown, Rehovot, where my family was waiting.

It has been less than an hour from Sinai and I'm already home, I thought.

We are really a small country.

We landed at Ben Gurion International Airport, the main civilian passenger airport in Israel, which was also used by the air force for cargo flights. Before this time, I had only been to the airport as a passenger going or coming from sightseeing trips to Europe or meeting friends arriving from abroad. It was strange to be back as a wounded soldier.

Four months earlier, though, I served at the airport for a month during a reserve stint. I was on call at the air force base adjacent to the civilian terminal for twenty-four hour periods every other day in case of a terrorist attack on the airport. Initiated after the murder of twenty-four people and the wounding of seventy-eight others by terrorists at the international passenger terminal in 1972, a military medical team was always at the ready in case of a repeat attack.

During that reserve tour, I became familiar with the passenger terminal. I made a daily trip from the miltary base in an air force ambulance through the airport's landing strips. We were instructed to practice daily the steps of a rapid response to a medical emergency in the civilian terminal. This necessitated requesting permission and crossing the main runway in the midst of takeoffs and landings.

Since I was actually not very busy during that month, I spent time writing letters and filling out applications for infectious disease fellowship sites in the United States, dropping the letters off at the airport's post office on my daily tours. Those letters were the ticket to my professional development. I was hoping to be able to pass through the airport on my way to the United States in a year as a result of these letters. On one of my daily trips I encountered a fellow physician who had graduated from my medical school a year before me and was on his way to a cardiology fellowship in the States. As I watched him, his wife, and their two children boarding the plane, I imagined myself doing the same a year later.

Ambulances waited for us when we landed and the injured soldiers were placed on them according to their destined hospital. I was sent to Beilinson Medical Center, about twenty kilometers away.

I knew that hospital well because I had completed my internship there five years earlier and my daughter was born there. I also knew many of the medical staff so I felt optimistic about being cared for by people I knew.

It was an unusual experience to leave the airport through a side gate instead of through Customs. As we drove out of the airport a giant C-5 U.S. Air Force cargo plane landed. As it touched down, it made a deep rumbling sound. It was good to see military supplies arriving. Witnessing how they were actually used on the front increased my gratitude to the United States for continuing to provide essential life-saving material. Watching the jet land also reminded me that I would be making the reverse trip within the next year to complete my medical training in America.

Knowing that I would be going abroad for a two year fellowship seemed even more appealing since it would allow my family a period of respite from the turbulent activity in the Middle East and its attendant insecurity. I also thought that being in the United States might give me the option to remain there and prevent my son from dying in a future mismanaged war. My experiences in this war had changed my perspective. I lost my trust in the ability of the Israeli leadership to act responsibly to ensure that soldiers won't lose their lives because their leaders had let their guards down.

The ambulance raced through the main highway blaring its siren. Other cars made way as we approached Beilinson Hospital. I was accompanied by two other wounded soldiers, each of whom had a cast on his hand. I noticed that traffic was lighter than usual, probably because so many men were away in the miltary. It seemed strange, however, to see that life was still going on while a bitter war was raging on two fronts. Of course I realized that things were not, in fact, the same as always; everyone was worried about family members and friends who were engaged in the war effort.

The ambulance took us directly to the emergency room, a place where I had spent the first month of my internship as a physician. It was strange to arrive at the familiar place as a patient. Several of the administrating staff and nurses remembered me and greeted me very warmly. I was placed in a treatment room and within a short time I was seen by Dr. Ibrahim, the Assistant Chief of the Department of Surgery. I had known him for over twelve years, as he was several years ahead of me in medical school. His brother, Halil, was in my medical school class and did his internship with me at Beilinson Hospital. I considered Halil to be one of my best friends. I assumed that Dr. Ibrahim had come to examine me because most of the other physicians in the hospital were in uniform while he, an Israeli Arab, was exempt from miltary service.

Dr. Ibrahim, whom I knew to be an excellent surgeon, was very proficient in caring for my leg wound. I greated him warmly but he seemed to be indifferent and distant. He seemed as though he had come to the emergency room against his will. After examining my wound carefully, he was able to remove the shrapnel and clean the wound thoroughly, leaving it open to heal without sutures. His attitude, however, continued to be very strange. He was cold and detached, never addressed me personally, and avoided eye contact. This was in contrast to the warm and friendly care I received from everyone else. My only explanation was that, as an Israeli Arab, his loyalties were with the countries fighting against us. Perhaps his attitude toward me was the same as I had toward the enemy soldiers I treated during the Six Day War – professional but not sympathetic. I never discovered an explanation for Dr. Ibrahim's behavior toward me. A few years later, though, I learned that he had become disgruntled with life in Israel and finally immigrated to the United States.

When the bandage from my left eye was removed I realized that my vision was still impaired. To make matters worse, the discoloration and swelling arround the orbit had intensified. I was then transferred from the general ward to the Opthalmology Department. After conducting several radiological studies, the doctors diagnosed a fracture in the zygomatic bone adjacent too my left eye. The bone was slightly dislodged from its normal position and the physicians decided to return the bone to its normal poition right away. They asked me to open my mouth and one of them manually pushed the bone into its correct position. The only upside to this painful proceedure was that it was very quick. The doctors explained that the dilation of my left pupil was caused by the trauma and that bleeding had developed after the bone was fractured. They predicted that my pupil would slowly return to its normal size within two to three weeks. They also diagnosed a whiplash injury in my neck that had also been caused by my head injury.

While being hospitalized I was like every one else, listening intently to the news. Now that I could no longer stop drivers in passing vehicles or experience the events myself, the radio and newspapers were my only source of information.

I learned that our forces had proceeded with their advance to the west side of the Suez Canal and had reached the city of Port Suez. They had surrounded the Egyptian Third Army and penetrated deeper into Egypt – only 101 kilometers from Cairo. Similarly, in the Golan Heights, Israeli forces had recaptured all the territory lost during the first days of the war and and were now only forty kilometers from Damascus.

After two days in the hospital, I learned that the fighting was finally over and a cease fire had been declared on both fronts. It seemed that Israel had not only escaped destruction but had also won militarily. The price, however, was very high. We suffered more than 2,800 dead and over nine thousand wounded during only 18 days of fighting. This was, indeed, a terrible cost felt everywhere in a small country whose Jewish population numbered only three million. The casualty rate was one death per thousand. At that time, I had no idea who had fallen. Doing the math, I feared that among the dead and wounded had to be some of my relatives and friends.

My head medic, Ehud, called me at the hospital to find out how I was doing. He told me that our battalion had crossed into Egypt and was still deployed there. Although we suffered several more casualties, at present things were quiet. Another physician had taken my place within a few hours of my evacuation and the medical needs of our battalion were being met. I was relieved to hear this. Even though I knew that someone would step into my shoes, I wanted to have this confirmed by Ehud.

He also updated me about the medical condition of David, our driver, who had been discharged from the hospital and was doing fine. Apparently he had not suffered a heart attack. Ehud had no information about the wherabouts of our other medic, Avner. Zvika's brother, who had been in a combat enginering unit, lost a leg. Althoughh Zvika learned about his brother's injury during the fighting, he did not leave the unit to visit him. I was proud when he told me that he stayed on with our medical team. Ehud also told me that our deputy commanding officer was going to recommend my promotion from the rank of Lieutenant (Segen) to Captain (Seren) and also recommended me for a citation because of the work I had done during the fighting. I was touched and grateful for the gesture.

I was happy when my wife, my two children and my sister came to visit the next day. It felt like I had not seen them for at least two months – not two weeks. So much had happened that it seemed as though I had been away for a much longer period of time.

I was in my hospital bed when they arrived. My wife and daughter were worried because my left eye was bandaged and the left side of my face was swollen. I tried to calm their anxiety by explaining the nature of my injuries and assured them that I would not suffer any permanent damage. Their worries intensified when I tried to get out of my hospital bed and walk, as they observed my bandaged left leg and my limping gait.

Eventually they seemed to be adjusting to my situation and my daughter told me about their experiences during the war. She told me that they had spent many hours in the bomb shelter, especially during the first week. She described how they had difficulties falling asleep at night and what games they had played during the long hours of being cooped up in a single room.

My wife brought me two letters that had arrived from the United States. They were from the heads of the two programs to which I had been accepted for fellowship training. One was from the program in Chicago that I had declined to accept and the other from the program in Los Angeles that I had agreed to accept. Upon reading the letters it was obvious to me that neither of the directors had received the letters I had mailed them two weeks earlier on Yom Kippur, the first day of the war.

The letter from Chicago, appeared to have been written in anger. The director inquired why I had not yet responded to the fellowship training offer, in effect scolding me for delaying my response and telling me this was an "unacceptable practice." There was no mention of the war raging in the region. The letter from Los Angeles did not even inquire if I had accepted the offer or not. It was just a letter of support and concern about our safety. The letter conveyed the concern of the program director and his wife and offered their support for our struggle. Even though both heads of the training programs were Jewish, their responses to our situation were very different. I could not understand why the Chicago program director did not realize that we were in the midst of a war and that mail services were not functioning as usual. After reading these letters, I immediately knew that I had made the right choice: I had selected a training program under a person who understood what we were going through.

Most of my friends were still stationed at the front, but my wife's cousin, Mexi, six years older than I, came to visit me at the hospital. Still wearing his uniform, he was on a two day leave from his military unit and, uncharacteristically, seemed very quiet and depressed. When I asked where he was during the war, I realized that he had been in the same division as I was. In fact we had been very close to each other during the fighting. In a voice barely above a whisper, he related his journey during the war.

He served as a medic, one of a team of seven in a tank battalion under Colonel Assaf Yaguri. The battalion had suffered heavy casulties attempting a counterattack against the Egyptians on the second day of the war. Although they were able to get very close to the Suez Canal, many of their tanks were destroyed by hand held anti-tank missiles. The tank crews, having had no prior knowledge, let alone experience with this kind of weapon, were completely unprepared. Many soldiers, including the commanding officers, were captured and taken prisoners of war by the Egyptians. Even though news about the devastating fate of this battalion had spread to our battalion during the war, I was not aware that Mexi was serving in that unit.

He recounted the grizzly sights he had seen and the devastation he encountered inside the damaged tanks. I could see how hard it was for Mexi to talk about his experiences and I did not press him to reveal all the details. He did, however, describe how difficult and painful it was to remove the bodies of dead tank crew soldiers from the tanks. Some of the dead were his friends whom he had known and with whom he had served for many years.

Miraculously, Mexi's medical team, including their physician, survived the fighting. Upon their retreat from the front, and despite their harrowing experiences, the entire medical unit was immediately reassigned to another tank battalion. They continued to serve until the last day of the war. No one seemed to appreciate what they had endured and the heavy emotional toll it had taken on all the medical team members, including my cousin. I gathered from his story and his demeanor that he and his team required immediate professional psychological assistance. Mexi recounted the nightmares and feelings of depression that he and other medics had suffered since their horrific experiences.

I was shaken by what I heard. I realized that my experiences paled in comparison to what Mexi and his friends, exposed to direct combat, had endured. I recalled the burned out tanks that I had seen during the war and realized that there were probably many other soldiers who had been exposed to similar horrific sights and experiences. It was clear to me that the plight of Mexi's unit was not being addressed by the military, even now that the fighting was over. Mexi was obviously too depressed to help himself or ask for assitance. I had to do something about it, but how could I do anything from a hospital bed?

Suddenly, it occurred to me that, as a physician in his division, I could refer him for medical and pschological care. I told Mexi that I strongly believed that he and his friends urgently needed psychological counseling to deal with their traumatic experiences. He did not need much persuasion to accept my suggestion.

I reached out for my military uniform still inside the night table. Fortunately, I was able to find the necessary military medical referral form in my shirt's pocket, and filled it out with the details and information Mexi provided. I also included a description of the psychological symptoms exhibited by the other members of Mexi's medical team. I asked him to take this referral letter to the military specialty clinic at Tel Hashomer Medical center so that he could get medical help as quckly as possible. I hoped the miltary medical system would respond promptly to address the impact of the psychological trauma that my cousin's team had endured.

Mexi quietly took my referral letter and promised to take it to Tel Hashomer hospital. As he left, I hoped that he would actually follow through. I was not sure if he would have the strength to overcome the stigma associated with seeking psychological help. I sensed, however, that he would comply, mainly because it was not only him that was suffering but also his entire medical team. I was also unsure whether the military establishment had the necessary tools to address the psychological trauma that they endured.

I was happy to learn from my wife that Mexi and his colleagues did receive help. Within days, the entire medical team was sent to a newly opened treatment program at the Wingate Village, an athletic school south of Netanya, where a building formerly used as part of the Gymnastics and Physical Education School had been converted into a psychological ward. Mexi told me that he and his friends were receiving treatment for two weeks, which included both individual and group therapy sessions. I later visited Mexi at Wingate and had a chance to meet the other members of his medical team; I sensed from talking to them how much they had gone through. Even though they seemed to be physically in good shape, most were abnormally quiet and introverted and I could feel their sadness. I couldn't tell whether their condition was a result of the medications they were receiving or whether it was due to their psychological trauma. Nevertheless, I appreciated the miltary for its efforts in helping Mexi and his unit. I hoped this intervention would help them.

After being hospitalized for five days I was finally discharged. On my first Saturday at home I went to the closest synagogue to recite the Gomel prayer. Somehow I was drawn back to the same tiny chapel I had passed about a month earlier on Yom Kippur as I made my way to the assembly site. On that day, seemingly so long ago, it had been filled with older men who would not be serving in the war. Now it was almost empty. It seemed that so much had happened since then. I teared up as I read the prayer in front of the ark. I felt lucky to have made it through alive. But as I stood there, practically alone in the house of worship, I felt a deep pain and sadness at the realization that so many had not made it alive of the war.

With the passage of time my vision slowly improved and my leg wound healed. Yet the scars and effects of the war were to stay with me forever.

Chapter 19
The Aftermath

When I returned home, I didn't feel the relief that I had expected. Instead, I felt shaken and depressed, feelings apparently shared by many others. My friends, neighbors, co-workers and even people in the street appeared sad and gloomy. Many wore strange expressions that seemed to be a combination of sadness, bewilderment, and disorientation. An atmosphere of shell shock prevailed, even though we were far from the front lines. People were walking with their heads bent down, their expressions gloomy. Very few smiled or joked. It felt like everyone was in mourning after a national disaster.

I actually observed a similar demeanor decades later when I visited Mexico City three days after a devastating earthquake in September of 1985 where more than ten thousand people died, and in the streets of Washington and New York City after the terrorist attacks of September 11, 2001 where more than three thousand people died. Apparently there is a universal reaction to tragedy as a society attempts to come to grips with a national calamity and loss of lives.

There was no celebration of victory, let alone a feeling of success as there had been after the Six Day War. Even though Israel was able to turn the tide of war after a surprise attack and then repel and soundly defeat its assailants, it did not feel like a triumph. The phrase, "One more victory like this and we will lose the war," expressed the general feeling. It felt as if the country had barely survived a traumatic event. For the first time since the 1948 War of Independence, there had been an imminent threat to Israel's very existence. I remembered how Winston Churchill had said that England could lose a battle but would not lose a war. In the case of Israel, one lost battle could have meant the loss of the war and thus the end of our existence. This war demonstrated our nation's inner vulnerability. I felt personally insecure and unsure whether I could even trust our leaders any longer. I understood that we could never again afford to fall asleep on "our watch."

No one knew what repercussions the war and its casualties would have on our future. There were so many dead and wounded. Just on our small street in Rehovot, with only twelve single houses and seven apartment buildings, there were two dead and seven wounded soldiers. Our apartment building, which housed only ten families, had one fallen and one wounded soldier. Seeing our elderly neighbors who had had lost their son and who lived a floor below us was difficult. Their grief was very deep and their pain evident in their faces and their demeanor. From the time the young man died, his mother and sister dressed in black and their faces bore deep sadness. Both lost weight and within a few months had became gaunt looking and pale. I never heard them laugh. Their apartment was very quiet and we never heard laughter or the sounds of music. Their lives had changed forever. Several months after losing his son, the father died from a heart attack.

I dreaded learning who of my friends and relatives had been wounded or died in the fighting. Over the next weeks I discovered that three of my friends died and four were wounded. The extent of the casulties was so great that the government published a book to catalogue the names of the dead. When the book was published a few months after the war ended I scanned the list of over 2800 dead soldiers with terror, fearing that I would find new names. I looked up names of friends I had not heard from to see if they were on the list. I discovered the names of two other people I knew on the list and I wondered how close I had been to having my name listed in the book. It would only have taken the shrapnel to hit me in the chest or head.

I continued to feel deep distrust and disappointment with the political and military leadership of the country. It was clear that hundreds of soldiers had to pay with their lives because the military reserves were not called up earlier. Compounding this error was the fact that many soldiers went to battle without the proper equipment and supplies. Israel was saved by those men who compensated for the lack of materiel with bravery and innovation. The word "courage" had a new meaning for me. I felt it was not an abstract concept, but instead was defined by the need to do what was necessary despite an inner fear.

I also was disappointed in the results of the diplomatic solution negotiated after a cease fire had been imposed on Israel. This was the result of the United Nations bowing to pressure by the Soviet Union, which had supplied and supported Egypt and Syria. Just as Israeli forces arrived at the gates of Cairo and Damascus, they were compelled to stop their advance. Complete victory, along with a chance to force our enemies to make peace, was snatched away in the last minute by politicians. The retreat from Egypt without forcing the Egyptians to abandon the east side of the Suez Canal was also unfair because it rewarded Egypt's agression. *We won the war. Why do we have to agree to terms that favor the defeated side?* I felt that by agreeing to terms forced upon us by US. Secretary of State Henry Kissinger, the government had ignored and desecrated the memory of the thousands who had fallen fighting to defend their country. I was expecting that Henrry Kissinger, the first Jewish Secretary of State of the United Sates to show more consideration for our nation's needs – and not force his policy on us.

After my discharge from the hospital and return home, I resumed the life that had been interrupted by war. I finished the last two months of my pediatric residency, and since I had six months left before I was to leave for the United States, began a fellowship in microbiology and infectious diseases at the Hadassah Medical Center in Jerusalem. I also worked as a physician at a Kibbutz south of Rehovot where I substituted for a medical school classmate still stationed with

Israeli troops in Egypt. However, I had no appreciation of what being in a war could do to a person's physical and emotional well being.

During the months after my injury I developed pain in my left elbow and arm. Although my symptoms were moderate and all the medical tests were negative, I was convinced that I was suffering from a serious and even terminal illness. I sought the help of the head of the department of neurology, one of my teachers at the medical school, who finally had a frank discussion with me. He explained that I was experiencing an irrational fear of death because of my recent war experiences. He had seen similar somatization of these fears in other injured soldiers, and explained that this reaction was due to the guilt of surviving the war while seeing others die. It felt good to be bluntly told that I was overreacting. By his directness, the doctor helped me overcome my anxiety.

In fact, the psychological effects of war had been evident within my own family. My uncle Aharon, my mother's brother, spoke throughout his life about his experiences during the Second World War. He had been a soldier in the Polish Army, a partisan, and later served in the Polish Army in exile fighting the Germans for six years. Whenever I saw him, it seemed to me that demons from his war experiences constantly hovered over him. He repeated again and again the same stories about his participation in battles against the Germans. I could not understand why he relentlessly recanted the same stories. Yet I only understood his behavior after having experienced war for only fourteen days. I could see how, by repeatedly reliving one's experiences and sharing them with sympathetic ears, one can slowly integrate and accept them.

I realized that this particular war would change my life forever. More fortunate than some of my friends and the many soldiers who gave their lives, I was lucky to have lived for many more years after the Yom Kippur War. Indeed, I always felt that I had been blessed with an extension of my life from the moment the rocket landed near me and almost killed me. It seemed that all the years that followed were a bonus to a life that could have easily ended at that moment.

My war experiences helped me deal with my mortality when I was diagnosed with throat cancer thirty-three years later. I told myself that I was fortunate to have been granted the time since my war injury to experience life in ways that I had not before. I was not ready to die at the time of the Yom Kippur War. I was only thirty-three years old and there was so much more that I wanted to do. More than three decades later, when I learned that I was suffering from throat cancer I was more ready to accept my mortality. After all, I had achieved many of the goals that I had set for myself when I was young. I took care of my two young children and then had three more; I experienced personal growth and relationships that enriched my life; and I was able to help many more patients, both through direct care and as a result of the research that I carried out or supervised.

In comparison to the war experiences of other soldiers who faced greater danger and saw many men die, mine were less intense. Nevertheless, these events affected me for a very long time. For over a decade I could not bear watching and listening to fireworks because they reminded me of artillery fire. The same was the case with the sound of thunder. The noise resonated in me and brought back the feeling of vulnerability that I felt during the war. When I joined my son to practice sharp shooting at a firing range nearly forty years after the war, I found the smell of gun powder and sounds of gun fire unnerving. I left the place as soon as I could.

I felt great disdain toward all weapons after the war. Even toy weapons annoyed me. I discouraged my children from playing with toy weapons and was appalled when I watched other youngsters having fun playing war games. Although I still believe that knowing how to use weapons appropriately and serving in the military may be essential for survival, I no longer find using weapons enjoyable or masculine. Although war may, at times and under certain circumstances, be necessary and inevitable, I have learned to hate it and find no glory in it.

My belief in the importance of weapons for self defense has not changed. Almost five years after the war, while living in the United

States, I learned first hand how important it was to know how to face an adversary and be ready to use a weapon. When a burglar broke into my house where my young children were sleeping, I challenged him with a pellet gun and held him at bay until the police arrived.

I stopped watching war movies for almost ten years after the war. When I resumed watching them I found out that many did not accurately reflect the atmosphere and reality of an actual battle. On the other hand, when I watched more realistic movies I could understand what the actors faced in a way that I could not have before. I almost always reflect on my own experiences when I watch war movies; in fact, to some degree, I find them almost therapeutic.

Now that I live in the United States, I'm still disturbed by costumes and decorations during Halloween that simulate physical injury. I am annoyed by children and adults who wear simulated blood-stained clothes, by manikins that are covered with "bloody" sheets, and by "amputated" blood-stained extremities that are used for celebrations. While the intention of these exhibits is to create an atmosphere of fun, I find them insensitive and upsetting. They seem to glorify the mortal injuries I faced during the war.

I never stopped talking about my war experiences over the years. Although over time the intensity of my emotions has diminished, the feelings themselves have not disappeared. Almost forty years later, many of the emotions I felt during the war are as vivid in my memories as they were on the day that I experienced them.

On my return home from the war I found Israeli society to be very receptive and supportive. The most therapeutic experiences for me were sharing my war stories with my friends who had also participated in the war and could appreciate what I had gone through. For hours on end, I recounted my own stories and listened to theirs. I realized that many of them had similar experiences to share. I recently shared my experiences with one of my old friends who had also served as a physician during the Yom Kippur War. To my amazement, I discovered that he served not far from me and that his war experiences and their aftermath were similar to mine. Finding out that my frustration, anxiety and fears were shared by many others made it easier for me to cope with them. Talking about the war experiences and reliving them again and again helped me to process and accept them. Eventually, I learned to live with my war memories.

Nine months after the war, I left Israel for my fellowship in the United States. I was unprepared to land in the midst of a society less understanding and supportive of what I had been through. Most people, including Jewish Americans, were polite and listened to the stories of my experience, but clearly could not appreciate the significance and magnitude of my trauma. It seemed to me that our country had endured an earthquake, while American Jews had been on stable land. This was a period of great anti-war sentiment in the United States because of the recently fought war in Vietnam. Many Americans seemed to allow their anti-war sentiment to cloud their response to Israel's struggle for its very survival.

In fact, the only sympathy and understanding of my war experiences came from American war veterans. Since the first year of my infectious disease fellowship was done in a Veterans' Administration hospital, many of my patients had seen combat themselves. Most were veterans of the Second World War, as well as the Korean and Vietnam wars. There were even a few elderly men who had served in the First World War. My recent war experiences made me very receptive and appreciative of what they had been through and I quickly discovered that most veterans were eager to share their own stories with me.

I remember one patient in his late fifties who was seriously ill with a foot infection. As I took his medical history he told me that he had injured his leg in the Battle of the Bulge in Belgium during the Second World War. He told me how ferocious the fighting had been and how many of his friends had been killed. Despite the fact that these events had occurred many years earlier, they were still very dominant in the man's mind and he was still dealing with them more than thirty years later. In a strange way I was comforted listening to these stories. I knew that these patients needed to keep talking. Those of us who have experienced war never stop processing our past.

The first time I found myself in a situation in which others could directly relate to, and appreciate, my war experiences was at Yom Kippur services exactly a year after the war.

We went to the Chabad Synagogue in Los Angeles. The rabbi began the services by reciting the events that had transpired a year earlier and emphasized exactly how close Israel had come to catastrophe. He asked the congregation to pray for the souls of the soldiers who gave their lives for the sanctity of God (Kidush Hasshem), thus saving Israel. I was moved to tears when I heard the rabbi speak. I felt I had finally found someone who understood what we went through. I realized that thousand of miles away from Israel there were Jews who truly shared our plight.

Unfortunately, I did not find such sympathy in other synagogues I attended at subsequent Yom Kippur services. After I moved to Washington, DC I attended a major synagogue where I naturally expected the Rabbis to mention during the Yom Kippur services what had transpired in Israel on that day. But the war was receding into history. Each year Yom Kippur passed without the war being mentioned. I could not feel any connection to a congregation that did not pay tribute to those who had fallen during the Yom Kippur War. I could not understand how Jewish people everywhere did not refer to the war in their Yom Kippur prayers and during the Martyrology. It was only after I contacted the rabbi that she consented to allow me to write and read a eulogy to the fallen soldiers on the twenty-fifth and thirtieth anniversaries of the war.

Once my infectious diseases fellowship ended, I remained in the States. The reasons for my stay were both personal and professional. My war experiences had little to do with the decision. However, my disappointment in, and mistrust of, the Israeli leadership who led the country at the time of the war made me reluctant to place my sons in the hands of irresponsible and negligent leaders. I continued to feel that way for at least ten years after the war ended. However, as my children grew older, I regretted my decision to let them become Americans and felt that they would have had a far better life and would have gained a richer Jewish identity in Israel, despite all of the obvious security issues.

I joined the medical corps of the United States Navy in 1980, seven years after the Yom Kippur War, mainly because of the research opportunities offered to me. As a naval officer, I found eager ears for my war stories and experiences. At that time I was one of a handful of physicians who had first hand experienced in war. Other officers looked up to me and asked my advice on practical issues related to mass casualties and PTSD. I delivered several lectures on these topics and shared my perspectives with Navy psychiatrists in training. I served 27 years in the Navy and always felt that I was serving the same cause, albeit in a different uniform. The memories of American assistance to Israel during the Yom Kippur War, including the ammunition boxes painted with the stars and stripes, the brown camouflaged American Phantom jet fighters painted with a Star of David, and the giant C5 Air Force cargo plane landing at Ben Gurion Airprt, made me feel that I was serving with a true friend of my homeland.

While in the Navy I qualified as a Marksman in both pistol and rifle. I accomplished this some eighteen years after the Yom Kippur War ended. With the passage of time the use of these weapons did not generate as strong a negative feeling in me as it had done initially. The Yom Kippur War taught me that even a physician needs to know how to defend himself.

For Jews who have lived through the Yom Kippur War, the holiest of the High Holy days will never be the same. For us, it stands not only as a day of atonement but as day of gratitude to God for the miracle of survival. It is also a time for remembering those who paid the ultimate price for preserving and protecting Israel, and will always commemorate a renewed commitment to preventing Israel from ever experiencing such a peril in the future.

ABOUT THE AUTHOR

Itzhak Brook, MD, MSc, is a Professor of Pediatrics at Georgetown University School of Medicine in Washington DC. He was born and raised in Haifa, Israel and graduated from the Hareali Haivri High School, earning his medical degree from Hebrew University, Hadassah School of Medicine, in Jerusalem. Dr Brook completed a residency in pediatrics at Kaplan Hospital in Rehovot, Israel. He served in the Israeli army as a battalion physician during the Yom Kippur war in 1973. Subsequently, he completed a fellowship in adult and pediatric infectious diseases at the University of California, Los Angeles, School of Medicine. Dr. Brook has authored several hundred publications in scientific journals and ten textbooks. He authored the book: "My voice - a physician's personal experience with throat cancer."